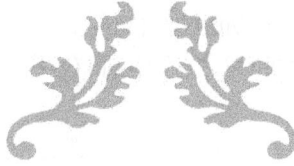

THANKSGIVING

MORE THAN A HOLIDAY FEAST

DAVID O. EKUNDAYO

THANKSGIVING: MORE THAN A HOLIDAY FEAST
Copyright © 2025 David O. Ekundayo

Request for further information should be addressed to:
THE KINGFISHERS INTERNATIONAL OUTREACH
www. info@kingfishersoutreach.org

ISBN: 9780954876364

Published by

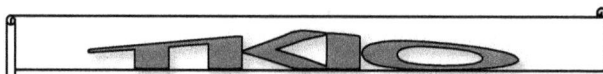

THE KINGFISHERS INTERNATIONAL OUTREACH

Making victors of victims; building a people of praise for God's end-time move

FOREWORD

In celebrating the First Thanksgiving in gratitude for a successful harvest that guaranteed their survival in 1621, the Pilgrim Fathers demonstrated their grasp of the concept of the feast that is now the cornerstone of the American society. However, Thanksgiving is more than a holiday feast.

The Bible exhorts us to "Oh, give thanks to the LORD, for He is good! For His mercy endures forever." Psalm 136:1 Therefore, thanksgiving is primarily about the goodness God shows to us and how we respond by showing our appreciation for His love and acknowledging His mercy, without which we cannot exist. Thanksgiving is, therefore, foundational to our existence and a subject worth studying in depth.

However, for most people, their understanding of thanksgiving is limited to a national holiday of festivities or a programme at Church to give thanks for God's love. Although both recognise God's goodness, they are not the only reasons we should thank God. This book seeks to offer irrefutable proof that thanksgiving is more than a turkey dinner and that it is not restricted to the four walls of the Church.

Thanksgiving is a divine command, a lifestyle, a celebration, a covenant, a seed for our victory, a medical remedy, a weapon of spiritual warfare, a compass for navigating the will of God, a conduit for appropriating God's promises, and a shield of spiritual protection that helps guide our lives toward the fulfilment of destiny, and a strategy for winning life's battles.

Those who thank God live their best lives. So, learn what it takes to be thankful in every sense of the word

TABLE OF CONTENTS

1. Thanksgiving: Anticipatory, Reflectory, and Celebratory 1

2. Thanksgiving And The Will Of God 23

3. Thanksgiving: Nurturing Your Seed Of Greatness 45

4. Weaponising Your Thanksgiving: How To Transform The Ordinary Into The Extraordinary 59

5. Thanksgiving: Strength Through Joy 85

1

Thanksgiving: Anticipatory, Reflectory, and Celebratory

'Thanksgiving' is a fundamental and operative word that means different things to different people. However, either as a national, congregational, or personal act of celebration, it is something we do that positively impacts us. It is therefore a great opportunity to delve deeper into this topic to gain a better understanding of why we should thank God.

The name gives it away. The import is that we give thanks to God as our primary object of worship. However, when discussing thanksgiving, the two other concepts that come to mind are praise and worship. There are technical differences between the three, but generally, people tend to use them interchangeably in the sense that whatever applies to thanksgiving also applies to praise and worship - they all operate on the same principles.

Hence, I won't be making technical differentiations, which implies that whenever I address thanksgiving, it also applies to praise and worship. So, what is the difference between praise, worship, and thanksgiving? We worship God because He is holy. Holiness is a specific and absolute attribute of God. Therefore, any other form of holiness derives from Him. Hence, we worship

God in the beauty of holiness as we acknowledge that He is worthy of our worship. He is a holy God. So, we worship Him.

We praise God for who He is - His excellent greatness, and because He is God. Our praise neither takes from nor adds to Him. It only acknowledges Him for who He already is. He is God and is worthy of our praises. So, we praise God for who He is.

We thank God for His goodness to us and for all that He has done in our lives. So, worship recognises the essence and holiness of God, praise acknowledges His character, and thanksgiving recognises the acts of God – His accomplishments in and around us.

Although I said I would not focus on the differences between all three and will thus lump them together as thanksgiving, it is worth noting that they all operate in a continuum, starting with thanksgiving, progressing into praise, and concluding with worship. The Old Testament Temple structure combines all three aspects of relating with God - we enter His gates with thanksgiving and access the courts of His presence with praise. Our worship is only possible as we acknowledge His presence and power in the Holy of Holies, where we commune with God.

Nevertheless, I will seek to differentiate between the three forms of thanksgiving to aid our understanding of the subject and help make sense of God's command to give thanks in everything.

Thanksgiving exists in three forms: reflectory, anticipatory, and celebratory. The character of our thanksgiving determines what we do with it, how it impacts our lives, and how we can leverage it in our quest to obey God's command to give thanks in everything. It is reflectory as you reflect on His goodness, anticipatory as you anticipate His greatness, and celebratory when you celebrate His blessings.

Reflectory thanksgiving involves taking time to reflect on and appreciate what God has done, like we do, for example, every New Year. We think of the old year - the things that have gone by, the challenges we have survived, and things we will change given the opportunity. Paraphrasing the French Philosopher René Descartes, who wrote, 'I think; therefore, I am'. We think, therefore, we thank, and in thanking God, we appreciate Him for who He is and what He has done for us. That is the essence of reflectory thanksgiving.

Anticipatory thanksgiving involves anticipating what God will do and projecting our thanksgiving into the future with a certain expectation of experiencing His goodness in recognition of His dependable character and the infallibility of His word.

Celebratory thanksgiving is the easiest of the three to define because it is the most common and comes naturally to us. For example, we routinely thank God for enabling us to see the New Year or month, and for every milestone and good thing that happens to us.

To further explain the concept of reflectory thanksgiving, I will cite a study by Professor Tony Campolo, a Christian sociologist, in which he formulated a question and presented it to a group of octogenarians and nonagenarians. He asked, 'If you have it to do all over again, what will you do differently?' These people were closer to the end of their lives than most. They had lived long and were being asked if they could change something about their lives, what would it be?

On collecting their responses and collating the results, the answers fell into three broad categories. The first group said, 'If I had it to do all over again, I would reflect more.' The second said, 'If I had it to do all over again, I would risk more'. The third group said, 'If I had it to do all over again, I would do something that would outlast me.'

Taking all three categories of responses together gives us an idea of how we should live our lives. While most of us are not yet 80 or 90 years old, if we can incorporate these answers into our lives, we will, in every way, lead highly productive lives, because all the things that we need to be thankful for are reflected in those answers.

The crux of their response is that by reflecting more, we get to realise and quickly correct our mistakes. It is because many people seldom reflect that they just live as if there's no end. Some people live as if they will never die. They behave as if death will never come. Some people are so taken over by power that they live as if there's no tomorrow. Once they attain power, you can no longer talk to them. They forget that power is transient. If only they could take time to think and say to themselves, 'Okay, I have this power today, but what will happen to me tomorrow if I no longer have it? If we can reflect in the fear of God, it will impact our subsequent actions.

Reflection helps us to identify and correct our mistakes and thus live more productive lives. These octogenarians and nonagenarians were living in regret and saying that if I had to live over again, if God were to give me 20 more years, I would do things differently. The good news for us is that by God's grace, we will live more than 20 years. So, we have time now to reflect and say, 'Okay, I've come this far. How did I get here? What could I have done differently? What are the roads I could have travelled and the roads I should not have? Why did I go this way when I could have gone that way?' This is what I will do differently in the future.

By responding, 'I would risk more', these sages were affirming that they would have less opportunity to regret either missed opportunities or opportunities not taken. Some opportunities come our way, but because we are fearful or unsure that it would work out, we decide not to take the risk and thus miss out. However, on reflection, we say to ourselves, 'Ah, if I have an opportunity like that again, I will risk it this time around, and the only way we can come to that conclusion is by reflecting.

So, we can take more risks because we are no longer overly cautious. Taking more risks on life's challenges and opportunities will enable us to get more out of life and make more difference. Willingness to take risks and correct our mistakes, means that we can live longer, learn, and benefit from our mistakes. It is the reason reflection is important and why taking risks and doing something that outlasts us matters.

Whenever some people reflect on their lives, it's all just about them - my house, my car, my career, my business. Never anything beyond them. And once you take them out of the equation, they have nothing left. They realise too late that success is best measured when in a team, or when you allow other people to succeed, and lift them to higher heights. It's not just about you alone. That was the truth these elderly respondents realised when they were already in their 80s and 90s. Had they applied that same truth in their 20s and 30s and throughout their lives, it would have had an impact on people around them. It would have impacted their marriages, businesses, their circle of friends, and every other aspect of their lives.

Therefore, we have the chance to look around at this moment and say, 'Okay, this is how far God has helped me. What can I do now to improve my relationship with this person or that person? Can I try to improve my marriage or myself? Reflection will help us to set our priorities and decide what truly matters.

Our primary challenge is differentiating between the unimportant and what matters. Somebody might have said something, and you didn't like it. So, you keep malice for many years, but does holding on to malice really matter or help to fulfil your destiny? If you realise that you only have five more years to live, would that malice still matter? No. You will overlook it and forget it ever happened because you know that in the larger scheme of things, it is unimportant. So, let's concentrate on enjoying ourselves and focus on working together to achieve something and leave a positive legacy.

By reflecting more, you can decide what matters and what is unimportant. Then, you focus your resources on what is important and do all you can with all you've got to attain the best results. The reason many of us live anyhow is that we seldom think of the impact our actions either on our own lives or on others. By reflecting more, we can review our past actions and make better decisions in the long term.

So, the simple truth is that these veterans, the 80 to 90-year-old people, have stated in a nutshell that we should be more thankful in our lives because when you reflect more and are thankful, you see things for what they really are. Yes, you have health challenges, but you're not dead yet. You may have financial challenges, but it is not the end of the world. God will make a way for you. Yes, you may have relational challenges. So what? God will turn things around for you. So long as you have life, you've got everything you need for life and godliness. You can thank God and start from where you are, so that you can end up where you want to be.

This fact is borne out by the Yoruba saying that those who know how to reflect also know how to give thanks. When you reflect, you can put everything in perspective. You don't allow things to get so overblown that they destroy the important.

Rene Descartes said, 'I think, therefore I am.' You think, then you become. Our problem is that we are too busy to think. We make ourselves too busy to spend quality time alone and think deeply about what is important, and because we rarely think deeply enough, when challenges come our way, we seldom know what is important for us or what is more important that we should hold on to, or less important that we should let go. Nevertheless, reflectory thanksgiving is something we can do just by looking at the past to help us situate our present and map out our future.

In comparison to more laid-back approach to reflectory thanksgiving, anticipatory thanksgiving is more proactive and therefore forward-looking because we require a form of thanksgiving that is both aggressive and creative. It is thanksgiving that involves the active deployment of faith, and all the risks that imply. With reflection, you can do nothing about the past. You can't change it, but you can own it and leverage it for your future. As somebody said, the past is a spent coin. Today is cash in hand. Tomorrow is just a promissory note. Nobody can guarantee that you will live to spend it. You can't change your past. All you have is today. So, spend it wisely.

Therefore, anticipatory thanksgiving involves taking the risk of faith with respect to shaping your tomorrow by thanking God today for a happier tomorrow. That's why we call it anticipatory thanksgiving.

John Wimber said, 'Faith is spelt R.I.S.K.' To walk by faith, you must take risks. Those old men and women understood that life is about taking risks, and said, 'Ah, if I have to live it all over again, I will take more risks. Where I had previously been too fearful, I now realise that there was no need to be fearful. If I had taken risk, I would have accomplished more. Therefore, to not risk is to court failure.

To love is to risk rejection but love all the same. Better to have loved and lost than never to have loved at all because of the fear of rejection. Nothing worthwhile in life is without an element of risk. Whenever you attempt to pursue success, you risk failure, but by saying that 'I won't attempt succeeding because I don't want to fail, you have already discounted yourself. You won't achieve anything. Thomas Edison said, 'A man who has never failed has never attempted anything.' That was the wisdom these sages were communicating. They were thinking, 'If only I could do this again, or if I had done that, things would have been different.'

We sometimes must risk rejection to experience love. That's when we gain the benefit of what it means to love or walk in love. So, taking the risk of faith involves staking our lives on God's word and saying, 'God, you have spoken. I believe it. I receive it. It is settled in my life.

Anticipatory thanksgiving means you already know what God's word says. So, you say, 'Lord God, because you are God, I thank you. I exalt you. I magnify you. I glorify you. I know you shall come through for me.' That's why the Bible says that in everything we should give thanks. But it also says in Philippians 4:6, 'Be anxious for nothing, but in everything with prayer, supplication, and thanksgiving we should make our request known unto God.'

Normally, thanksgiving or thanking someone only comes after something has been done for us, and we show our appreciation by saying, 'Thank you'. For example, we can say, 'Thank you, Lord God, for providing me a house.' 'Thank you, Lord God, for providing me with food.' 'Thank you, Lord God, for good health.

For those blessings you are already enjoying, your thanksgiving is either celebratory or reflectory. You thank God for all He has done by saying, 'Lord, I bless you for what you've done. I give you praise. I celebrate your goodness.'

However, when you thank God before those things you asked for have physically manifested, but in anticipation that they will be fulfilled in the fullness of time, that is anticipatory thanksgiving. Apostle Paul wrote in Philippians, 'Be anxious for nothing, but in everything with prayer, supplication and thanksgiving....'

When facing challenges, God says, 'Don't worry. Don't be anxious. Just pray.' You supplicate and ask God. God said, 'Ask of me, and I will give you whatever you ask for. Call on my name, and I will answer. God says, Ask, because only those who ask receive. Those who seek find, and those who knock, the door shall be opened unto them. Mattew 7:8 Jesus Christ said that if you ask anything of the Father in His name, He will do it. John 14:13-14 If we ask anything of the Father in His name, we should know that He hears us, and because we know He hears us, we give glory to God in anticipation of receiving the answer.

Even though you haven't seen what you're asking God for, you can still say, 'Thank you, Lord.' Why? Because you know that God has answered you as stipulated by His word. Hence, you are thanking God by faith, because faith believes and then receives. It is being sure of what we do not see and certain of what we are still expecting. So, that is anticipatory thanksgiving.

For example, at the beginning of each year, we thank God by faith even though we don't know what challenges the year may hold for us. What we do know is that whether the year is wonderful or not, God is still God. He remains worthy of our thanksgiving. His word is still the same. He does not change and will never lie. He is still worthy of our praise. We still need to thank Him for the fact that we are alive.

So, by thanking God in anticipation, we project our faith into the future and leverage His power to shape that future. We say, 'Lord God, I thank you because I know that you will take care of me'. That's just it. So, you know that whenever issues crop up, you will pray and still thank God in anticipation of His resolution. So, we are thanking God for the past, the future, and the present.

Celebratory thanksgiving involves showing appreciation to God for what He has done, usually recently, but also in the past. It is when we share our testimony, 'God has done this for me, or God has done that for me, and I thank Him.' Maybe you've been experiencing difficulties, and God answers your prayer and blesses you. Of course, you will thank Him.

Of the three forms of thanksgiving, the most difficult is anticipatory thanksgiving. The easiest to do is celebratory thanksgiving. It is a given to thank God whenever God blesses you, for thanking God comes naturally when life is good. This was the crime Satan accused Job of committing. He said accusingly, 'Of course, why will Job not worship you? See how blessed he is. Look at his children; they are blessed. His business is growing and doing well. Look at the man, he is even fat. Why will he not worship you?

Hence, it's natural to worship God when things are good and more challenging in difficult times, but because God is God when we are on the mountain top and the same when we are in the valley, we praise and thank God all the time. That's why David said, 'I Will Bless the Lord at all times; His praise shall continually be in my mouth. Psalm 34:1 It is the reason Apostle Paul could write, 'In everything, give thanks, for this is the will of God for you in Christ Jesus', proving that thanksgiving is what God expects of us.

Thanksgiving should be an attitude which guides our actions and not just restricted to actions. It is the same reason this principle applies to praise and worship as well.

Many people think worship is something you do only within the four walls of the church, but God says that He is seeking those who would worship Him in spirit and in truth. John 4:23 So, worshipping God should be an attitude, something that comes from deep within us and that we do anywhere. We must become worshippers in everything that we do. So, driving the car constitutes our worship to God. Eating is worshipping God. Everything we do is worship. So, it cannot be restricted to just the four walls of the Church or be designated as a 'Thanksgiving Service'. Your entire life should be a praise to Him. The Bible says that He has called us out of darkness into His marvellous light, but to do what? To show forth His praise. 1 Peter 2:8

Hence, our thanksgiving should transcend our actions and become a way of life. It is about us 'being' before 'doing'. Being 'human beings' is what makes us who we are and determines what we do.

So, when you cultivate a heart of thanksgiving, you always see a reason to give thanks to God in everything, especially when facing difficulties. It was the reason Habakkuk could say, 'Though the fig tree does not blossom ......and there are no cattle in the stall...' Those are difficult situations. His response, however, was, 'Yet, I will praise God. I will give thanks to the God of my salvation.' Why? Because God is good, God is great all the time, not some of the time.

So, how do all the three forms of thanksgiving, that is, reflectory, celebratory, and anticipatory, dovetail into each other? It simply means that God expects us to always be thankful. Reflecting on God's goodness opens the doors of our lives to God's favour to give us what we need. A thankful heart attracts God's favour and shuts the enemy out of your life. He will frustrate the enemy's attempt to distract you.

Remember Job. After the worst thing that could happen to any man had happened to him, the Bible says, 'And Job bowed down and worshipped God.' He said, 'Lord, I thank you. Naked I came into this world, naked I will depart. Lord, I give you all the glory, I give you all the honour. I know that my life is in your hands.' And because Job worshipped God in his distress, the enemy could not get him. It would have been a different matter if Job had complained or rebelled against God. He would have opened his life to the enemy and would have been destroyed.

So, reflectory thanksgiving means that even if we admit past mistakes as we reflect and thank God for His goodness, God can speak to us. He will say, 'Come on, forgive that person.' 'Oh, do this or do that.' Heeding God's word will raise you up to where you're supposed to be and foil Satan's attempt to drag you down.

When you consider the story of Joseph and his horrible experiences, do you think it was easy when he laid eyes on his brothers, the ones who had sold him into slavery and nearly killed him? He was so overcome with emotion that he broke down in tears. Maybe, and it's something that I've experienced, you think you have already forgiven somebody, that was until they stepped back into your life, and everything just comes rushing back - the pain, hurt, etc. That was how Joseph felt, and what did he do? He retired to his inner sanctum and cried his heart out.

Joseph felt the urge for revenge to repay the ills his brothers had done to him in their own coin but also knew that vengeance was God's. Instead, he asked for grace and prayed, 'Lord, help me to love my brothers', and God answered his prayer. Joseph reflected on the situation and saw God's hand in his life. He concluded as he confronted his brothers, 'You intended to do evil to me, but God meant it for good.'

Reflectory thanksgiving enables you to see the bigger picture and reach that level where you're able to forgive and forget and move on with your life. Why? Because as you reflect and thank God, you can stay within the will of God for your life and experience the favour of God. This confirms the Yoruba saying that an appreciative child is always guaranteed his father's future favours. Why? Because gratitude attracts favour.

Therefore, closing the virtuous cycle of thanksgiving requires that we always thank God in anticipation of His goodness, since anticipation always precedes fulfilment.

The word 'Anticipate' means to expect that you will receive what you hope for. Job's response to his calamity was, 'What I have feared has come upon me', proving that whatever you expect is indeed what you attract into your life. So, through anticipatory thanksgiving, we make room for God in our lives as we anticipate what God will do, as our fear of God attracts His favour into our lives.

The reality is that whatever you are expecting will never take you by surprise. Why? Because you already know it is coming. Through thanksgiving, we exchange our fears of what Satan, man, or circumstances can do to us for faith in God's unparalleled ability to care for us and prosper us regardless of circumstances and thus set us on the course of God's plan to bless us.

After you've prayed effectually, you are no longer anxious, because God's peace alights on you. You've prayed, supplicated, and thanked God. You know that God will give you understanding that enables you to know that, because I have prayed and believe, blessings are coming my way.

The peace that comes from knowing that God has your back influences your outlook and shapes your behaviour. People may wonder, 'I thought you said you had a problem.' You will respond, 'Yes, I did, but it is in the past now. I no longer have a problem because my God is resolving it. I'm just waiting for the solution to appear.'

Our positive and expectant mindset based on God's faithfulness means that we can dare to celebrate in anticipation of the fulfilment of His promise to us. So, whenever something bad happens, instead of complaining, we will rather say, 'God, I bless you because I have the victory. My victory is coming, it hasn't yet arrived, but I know it is coming.' So, you start praising God.

Hence, what should your strategy for living a thankful life be?

1. **Start from where you are**. There is no better time or place to start thanking God than in the present. Don't say, I will wait until things improve before I start thanking God. If that were the case, you've already negated God's injunction in Philippians 4:6, which says, 'Be anxious for nothing; but in everything with prayer, supplication and thanksgiving.' It says, 'In everything'. So, don't just wait there, thank God! In Psalm 104:33-34, David wrote, "I will sing to the Lord as long as I live; I will sing praise to my God while I have my being. May my meditation be sweet to Him; I will be glad in the Lord." So long as you are alive, praise God, bless His name, and give thanks to God, because that is the measure of your faith in Him that He will do as He promised.

   Psalm 126:6 states that those who go out carrying seed with weeping shall doubtless return with songs of joy, bringing in their sheaves. Whenever you sow your seed of thanksgiving, you can be confident of reaping a harvest of the joy of the Lord in the fullness of time.

2. **Start with what you have, however small it may be.** Zechariah 4:10 states, "For who has despised the day of small things? For these seven rejoice to see the plumb line in the hand of Zerubbabel. They are the eyes of the LORD, which scan to and fro throughout the whole earth." So, start from where you are, and with what you have. Don't say, 'I will thank God when my blessing gets up to a certain level.' Start from where you are. Count your blessings, name them one by one. Maybe

16

you can only name five today, focus on those five and start thanking God for what you have. Before long, He will pour His blessings on you and you will be thanking God for 50 additional blessings, and then reach a point where you say, 'God, I can't even count them all anymore.' Start with what you have, however little you have, and bless God, for though your beginning is small, your latter end shall be great indeed.

Remember what Jesus Christ did when He fed the 5,000? He challenged His disciples, 'Go and feed the people', and the disciples responded, 'Sir, are you mad? Feed 5,000 people? With what? Where are we going to find food in this deserted place? Jesus was only testing their faith. He already knew what He wanted to do. He was only saying, 'Look around, see what you have', and they were able to bring Him two loaves and five fish. Jesus Christ blessed it, and then what happened? It expanded, multiplied, and fed 5,000 people, with something left for the original giver.

Whatever it is that you have, consider it a seed. The principle of increase is that whatever cannot sufficiently feed you is but a seed to sow. Whatever you have that cannot fully meet your need is a seed to sow to reap a harvest of abundance down the line. Sow your seed and God will multiply it. It will grow, reproduce its kind and produce fruit. You eat the fruit but sow the seed.

3. **Be thankful for what you have instead of focusing on and griping about what you lack.** This is the main reason many of us get into

trouble and are so miserable. The Western World should, in terms of material wealth, have the happiest people in the world. They have cars and houses and go on holidays as if it is out of fashion; things that should make them the happiest people on earth. However, whenever a survey is conducted for the happiest people, the winners are usually countries that are relatively materially deprived, where some don't even have a roof over their heads. Why? It is because we've reached the stage where we feel too entitled and are no longer thankful for or satisfied with what we have. Our focus is usually on what God has not done and the things we lack, when we should be thanking God for what He has already done in anticipation of what He will do next. Our prayer should be, 'God, I may not be where I want to be, but I thank you that I'm no longer where I used to be.'

There is a saying that a bird in hand is worth two in the bush. When you are thankful for what you already have and value the little that you have, you will see God pouring His grace upon your life. Hence, being thankful instead of griping will guarantee God's presence in our lives, proving that godliness and contentment is great gain.

4. **Understand that the very things you take for granted constitute the unfulfilled and greatest heart desires of others.** For example, you may look at your 2-year-old car and complain, 'I don't like this car anymore', and put it up for sale. What you no longer want is what other people will rush to snap up because it meets their needs. The reason you must be thankful is that many people don't yet have the things you

have and have taken for granted. Whatever you have - good health, happiness, children, etc. Just say, 'Lord God, I thank you for all you have given me.'

You have so many reasons to give thanks to God, the starting point of which is your life. Only the living can praise God. Hence, you can't say I don't have any reason to thank God. You have a lot to thank God for. If you truly reflect and think deeply, you will have the opportunity to look around and see what is missing in the lives of people around you that you don't even think about because it's never been an issue with you.

You only know how blessed you are as you face challenges in specific areas of your life that you had previously taken for granted. The importance of being healthy only comes into focus when you are struggling with health challenges and things are not working as they normally should. Feeling pains on your fingertips makes you appreciate the fortitude of somebody experiencing pain from the crown of their head to the tip of their toes. Ence, understand that we have no reason to complain if we have no shoes to wear, because somebody out there has no legs to walk on. You will always have a reason to thank God; you only need to find it.

Finally, who should give thanks? Anyone and everyone. Thanksgiving is neither time-bound nor exclusive. It is a lifetime venture that is open to everyone. You can be reflectory, anticipatory or celebratory at any stage in life, and preferably at all stages of your life. The earlier you start thanking God, the better. You don't have to be 80 or 90 years old before you start reflecting. If you plan to leave a good legacy, start thanking God and cultivate a attitude of thanksgiving when you are in your 20s, 30s, 40s and 50s, when you still have time to grow and can still make changes, and you will see the glory of God in your life.

Understand that ability to reflect comes with age, experience and teachability. You are more likely to reflect more as you grow older, because experience means that you have been there, done that, and hopefully learned something. You will have your joys and regrets and therefore have more materials to work with and the capacity to look back and see things from the perspective experience gives you, and you will reflect more. A younger person who sees the world as their oyster may see little need to reflect because they are yet to make their mistakes. Hence, it may be easier for the older person to reflect, but I can assure you that younger persons who start reflecting earlier in life will make more headway than those waiting until they are old and grey to start reflecting. So, I encourage you to reflect more.

Nevertheless, reflection, like meditation, needs to be done in a certain way. It must be scriptural. Don't just reflect using the standards of the world. Let your reflection be godly rather than worldly. So, base your reflection on God's plan for your life relative to your achievement. Never compare yourself with somebody else, because you have different destinies. Don't say, 'My brother or my sister or my friend has got this house, they've got that business, what about me? You must reflect based on God's word to you in line with His will for your life. You ask, 'God, what is your will for me at this stage of my life?'

If God's will is for you to have a house at this time, and you don't yet have one, then bully to you. Go and get a house.

Effective reflection requires you to use God's term of reference and follow His purpose for your life. As you reflect, you will think more about the good things. The Bible says, "Finally, brethren, whatever things are true, whatever things are noble, whatever things are just, whatever things are pure, whatever things are lovely, whatever things are of good report, if there is any virtue and if there is anything praiseworthy—meditate on these things." Philippians 4:8 Why? Because 'As a man thinks in his heart, so is he.' Proverbs 23:7 When you reflect more, think more, and are therefore more thankful, you will experience more of the grace of God in your life.

Anticipation, or hope, or expectation is a quality unique to the living, which informs the saying that where there is life, there is hope. You can thank God because you're alive. Some people thanked God only 5 days ago; they can't anymore because they are gone. So, if you are alive, give glory to God.

While reflection can sometimes lead to regret, hope gives us impetus to correct our mistakes and invest in a better future that we might not even see. Sometimes you do things just because it is the right thing to do, not because we will personally benefit from it, but it will benefit those who come after you. When you do the right things and lay a solid foundation in anticipation of things you will not see, that is what you call an excellent spirit.

Abraham time on earth was limited, but he lived to benefit a posterity that he would not physically live long enough to see. This means that we can project our lives and faith beyond our own lives. So, being thankful makes you ultimately significant.

So, given the constraints of time, anticipatory thanksgiving implies thanking God for an end that you may not physically see, but which you have already seen by faith, and thus call things which are not as though they were, thereby declaring the end from the beginning.

In conclusion, in everything, give thanks, for this is the will of God for you in Christ Jesus. So, thank Him by your reflection on His goodness or in the anticipation of faith in His ability to deliver on His promise to you, and if God has done it, in celebration of His excellent greatness. Whatever your situation, give thanks!

2

Thanksgiving And The Will Of God

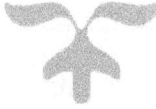

"In everything, give thanks, for this is the will of God for you in Christ Jesus."
1 Thessalonians 5:18

In the English Language, the word 'Everything' means all-encompassing. Nothing is exempt. The Bible enjoins us to give thanks in everything, but we also understand that it is a bit difficult to practise.

It is easy to give thanks when something wonderful happens to you. You come to church and give thanks because it is a joyful occasion. It is good to give thanks, and we do it naturally when good things happen to us. However, when things go the other way, it can be a bit difficult giving thanks. We would rather do the opposite and complain because we are human beings.

Hence, in this chapter, we will explore this topic to see how it relates to the will of God for our lives, for it says, 'In everything, give thanks, for this is the will of God for you in Christ Jesus.' So, if thanksgiving is the will of God for us in Christ Jesus, then it means that we should give thanks in everything, good or bad. But why can this be difficult? It is because it is a radical and counterintuitive way of thinking and lifestyle. How can you give thanks in everything when you know that as a human being, it's nigh impossible not to complain, especially in tough times? We will address this issue by examining the 10 ways thanksgiving helps to keep you within God's will, thereby enabling you to fulfil destiny.

We will start by asking, what is a will? A will is a legal document stating your desires or what you want done with your property. In the United Kingdom, you are required to have a will if you have substantial property holdings, so that you can determine who receives what after you are gone. Dying intestate, that is, without leaving a will, means that the government will step in and decide the manner of distribution of your estate. To avoid that, citizens are always encouraged to have a will.

Whenever you want to execute a will, let's say of an individual, it usually states, 'This is the last will and testament' of the named individual. It outlines a set of instructions for its executors to fulfil the wishes of the writer.

God also has His written will: the Old Testament and the New Testament. So, God's will is His word. This means that the first place we need to look to find God's will is His word. Why? Because He has already outlined His desire in His word. So, if you are seeking to understand what God's will is and don't know where to begin, start with the word of God. Usually, the best way to know God is getting into the Word, knowing what He likes and what He doesn't. That is how you know what we call the general will of God.

The general will of God is represented by the general knowledge of God as gained from the *logos* or the written word of God. So, anytime you pick up your Bible and you are reading and seeing the interaction of God with different people, and He is stating, 'This is what I want, this is what I will punish, etc, you're able to know that this is what God loves, and this is what He hates.

For example, concerning marriage, God says a man shall not lust after another person's wife, but you see a married woman walking across your path, and say, "I like that lady." The will of God will tell you, "Ah, that's forbidden." So, you know the general will of God in that way, but also understand the specific will of God, too, because God's will can be general as well as specific.

Some instructions are general - don't steal or commit adultery, but finding out God's will about your impending journey to the City of Birmingham is specific and applies only to you. God could say, 'Go or don't go to Birmingham tomorrow. That is a specific instruction to you.

How do you know the will of God? It is through the word of God. By interacting with the word, you get to understand God's will. So, what is God's will? God's will fall in two parts: the established will and the revealed will of God.

The established will of God is represented by the Old and New Testaments of the Bible. These tell us what God requires of us, and which will not change because of circumstances. Hence, once the will of God is known, it applies for all time and to all people without exception. It is set in stone because it is a fact; nothing can change it.

However, there is also the revealed will of God that builds upon what has already been established and comes to the fore as we walk with God. The way I like to describe it is by using the example of you travelling from London to

Birmingham for the first time. Since you have never been to the City of Birmingham before, you will join the M1 and will periodically see signboards announcing Birmingham 100 miles, 50 miles. The distance of travel decreases as you get closer. You know that you are getting closer to Birmingham even though you've never been. However, the moment you arrive in Birmingham, you no longer need the direction sign. You have arrived!

The established will of God is like a signboard announcing that Birmingham is 100 miles away. The specific or revealed will of God is the signpost welcoming you to Birmingham. It is God speaking directly to you, saying, 'This is what I want for you.' Both the established will of God and His revealed will represent God's plan for your life.

1. Therefore, the first lesson about thanksgiving regarding God's will is that **God's will is the safest place in the world**. Understand that anything outside of God's will also falls outside the protection of His grace. The key principle is that God's will or God Himself will not lead you into a situation where His grace cannot cover you. Walking in God's will guarantees that God will take care of you. Even when God leads you into trouble, so long as you recognise it is His will, you can trust that God has a plan. He will either deliver you from that trouble, or if He chooses not to, you can still be confident that you are within God's will and supported by Him.

   So, the reason we must do God's will at all times is because it is the best place we can ever be; we are always under God's direct jurisdiction, where the enemy can do his worst but God will still bring His best out of it and cause all things to work together for our good because we love Him. So, when the Bible says that in everything, give thanks, it is because God knows that when you strive to do His will, you also get to a place of safety.

So, regarding God's injunction to give thanks in everything as God's will, the reason you must seek to do God's will, even when things are difficult and you feel like complaining, is that anything you do that takes you out of God's will only take you further away from the safety His presence provides.

2. Second, **thanksgiving guides or dovetails you into God's perfect will.** When you thank God in everything, you can never go wrong. Sometimes, when things go wrong, contrary to our expectations, instead of acting rashly and emotionally, you simply say, "God, I don't understand what is going on, but I still thank you all the same because I know that you have good plans for me. You will cause all things to work together for me." Your positive attitude will allow God to take charge of the situation and lead you into His perfect will for your life.

When Job heard the calamitous news that he had lost everything, instead of shouting and castigating God for His failure to protect him, Job simply bowed down and said, "Naked I came from my mother's womb, And naked shall I return there. The Lord gave, and the Lord has taken away; Blessed be the name of the Lord." In all this Job did not sin nor charge God with wrong." Job 1:21-22 In his most difficult hour, instead of getting angry with God because something untoward happened to him, Job chose to worship God and demonstrate submission to His will.

We sometimes get angry with God when we face unexpected challenges, and some of us respond by turning our backs on Him and lashing out at God. In essence, we are blaming Him for our predicament. This is a natural response to calamity that drives us further from God and into Satan's waiting arms. The supernatural response that meets God's approval and never fails to secure His backing is to choose to honour God in our difficulties by saying, "God, I'm in pain right now, but you're still God. I entrust my life to you."

God's response to your loving attitude towards Him in your difficult situation would be to direct your heart towards what is good. Regardless of the severity of your predicament, thanksgiving will always lead you into God's presence, and not away from Him, seeing as you enter His gates with thanksgiving and His court with praise. Psalm 100:4

Hence, thanksgiving always guides you into God's perfect will for your life. Psalm 50:23 states, 'Whoever offers praise glorifies me, and to him who orders his way aright will I show the salvation of God', proving that God is always waiting for us to praise Him, so that He can respond and show His salvation to us.

Jeremiah 33:3 says, "Call upon me and I will answer you, and I will show you great and mighty things that you do not know." But how will

God show you His salvation or answer you if you are so angry with Him that you turn your back on Him? How can you call upon a God you are cursing in your heart for help?

So, thanksgiving is not just about how you feel; it is you saying, "God, I choose to obey." If it is indeed true that thanksgiving is how I receive the will of God, in this case, I choose to obey you regardless of how I feel. I will praise, exalt, and magnify your name because I know that you are on my case. Hence, thanksgiving dovetails and guides us into the will of God for our lives. Anything else will either push us away from Him and completely out of His will or into His permissive will.

God's will fall into three categories – perfect, permissive, and against His will. Any response to difficulties other than thanksgiving will either push us out of His perfect will, and into His permissive will, or entirely out of His will. The latter two do not represent God's best for us.

3.   Third, **thanksgiving leads us into God's perfect will for our lives**. His perfect will represents what God really wants for us. His permissive will is what we want for ourselves, regardless of what God wants for us, which He nonetheless allows as He adjusts His plans for us to suit His agenda. However, this option often has unforeseen repercussions, as it proved for the Israelites when they demanded meat in the wilderness. God gave them what they wanted, but it brought leanness to their soul. Psalm 106:15 So, God's perfect will is ultimately always the best for us.

Many of us either deliberately or unwittingly get ourselves into situations that God didn't want us in because of our wrong attitude and mindset, or because we think we are wiser than God. That was the *faux pas* the Seer Balaam committed. He had approached God and requested, 'Let me go and curse the Israelites'. God's firm response was, 'No.' However, motivated by his greed, Balaam persisted in his request until God allowed him to go.

Whenever we think we are wise and seek to dictate to God, He will give ground and allow us to be caught in the snare of our own foolishness. That comes with grave repercussions and consequences unforeseen by us. As Balaam was going to curse the Israelites, the Bible says that the angel of God ambushed him and wanted to kill him. He was only saved by his donkey, which refused to move at his command.

Then, the angel of God forced Ballam to only say what God commanded him. He was to bless the Israelites. So, Balaam went from receiving the perfect will of God to executing His permissive will and ultimately ended outside the will of God by joining effort with Israel's enemies to sabotage God's plan.

An even worse situation is to go from being in the centre of God's will and ending up outside His will. An example of someone who took this near-fatal turn was David. God had anointed David the presumptive king of Israel after rejecting King Saul, and David thought everything would be just fine. Instead, all hell broke loose. However, because David was not expecting things to become difficult, as Saul was trying to kill him, it got to the point where David could no longer take the pressure. So, one day, David got up and thought to himself, 'The way things are going, one day Saul will get me.' The lies we tell ourselves.

Just months earlier, this same Saul came to Naioth, a campground where David and Samuel were praying, to arrest David. 1 Samuel 19 Instead, God arrested and detained Saul in His presence, and he prophesied from morning till night, allowing David to use the opportunity to effect his escape, and Saul could not harm him.

Sometimes, tough circumstances cause us to take our eyes off God, because we do not always feel strong. We can even become depressed, and in that state of impaired judgment, start making decisions that are not right for us. However, even in those cases, one way to prevent ourselves from going down the wrong path is through thanksgiving. We bless and honour God to secure His help.

David exemplified this response in Psalm 42:5, by saying, "Why are you cast down, O my soul? And why are you disquieted within me? Hope in God, for I shall yet praise Him for the help of His countenance." He recognised the way out of depression and practised it. We should emulate him.

I had a similar experience when I first moved to the United Kingdom. Things were tough for me as a new immigrant, as I am sure many will understand. Although things were hard for me, it really did not negatively impact me because I was joyful, focused, and always serving God. I always had a smile on my face.

Then, one day, I took my eyes off God and focused on my circumstances and became disheartened. I was working but couldn't pay my rent. I couldn't buy the necessities because I was always short of money. I remember I couldn't stand straight in the only pair of shoes I had because the rubber soles were worn at the heels. So, I began asking myself and querying God, what kind of life is this? I've been serving you, yet nothing is happening. I turned my back on God and consequently became depressed.

Normally, I would head for Church every Sunday morning to open the doors and get everything ready for service, but not this Sunday. So, I told my friends to go without me. I had no intention of attending the service because I was angry with God. Instead, I jumped in bed and hid under the duvet cover.

Everything went quiet in the house. Then God spoke and asked me, 'David, what are you doing here?' I felt like a deer caught in the glare of headlights. I knew how Elijah must have felt when God asked him the same question after Elijah had asked God to kill him, but unlike Elijah, I had no cogent answer. A feeling of guilt swept over me as I realised that I should not be here! I felt as if God had caught me red-handed doing something wrong.

God did not say anything more, but He didn't have to. I knew that I was supposed to be in church praising God, not lying complainingly on my bed. I had no business being depressed because of my difficult circumstances, and I recognised why. I had made a fundamental mistake and taken my eyes off God and instead focused them on my circumstances. Depression or not, I felt an urge to apologise to God for letting Him down and promised that if He got me out of the pit of depression I was then ensnared in, I would never be depressed again in my life.

God answered my prayer and helped put things in the right perspective for me. He drew me out of the miry clay of depression and taught me how to stay out of that slimy pit. Since then, I have been in even more difficult circumstances, but by His grace, I have never again been depressed, and that was over thirty years ago. I now know what to do to avoid getting depressed – I give thanks in everything.

From that experience, I learned the lifelong lesson that there are some paths God never intended for you, and you should never walk. You must do your utmost and avoid such paths, because they are a rabbit hole. As David's Ziklag experience proves, such paths will lead you out of God's will and into harm's way, where Satan can attack you. I also learned that sticking to God's word to give thanks in everything, however costly, would have saved me from such an experience

Hence, thanksgiving is like a gate we shut to stop us from going where we shouldn't, thereby safeguarding ourselves in the will of God.

Whenever we thank God, God will speak to us, saying, 'Stop! Don't go there. Don't think that way. Focus on me.' will get through to us, because thanksgiving makes us receptive to hearing His word.

So, by thanking God, you avoid seeing things that your eyes should not see, but which Satan wants you to focus on to discourage you. I have since understood that there's a reason for it whenever God says, 'In everything, give thanks.' It stops you from going where you shouldn't, so that your eyes don't see what you shouldn't.

So, through thanksgiving, you empower God to maintain the initiative and perfect His work concerning your life. Psalm 138:8 "The LORD will perfect that which concerns me; Your mercy, O LORD, endures forever; Do not forsake the works of Your hands."

We are all works in progress, not finished work, and sometimes when God is working on us, things can become very difficult for us. By being thankful, you are saying, 'God, I know that your plans for me are good. I know that you will cause all things to work together for my good.'

Our ingratitude sometimes hampers God from doing what He desires to do for us. So, understand that whenever you choose to thank God in your difficulties, God is working and perfecting that which concerns you.

4. Fourth, **thanksgiving enables you to avoid foolishness.** Foolishness is different from being a fool. Foolishness depicts the wrong action of a person, while being a fool shows the flawed

character of that person. That is an important differentiation. The Bible defines a fool as someone who maintains that there is no God and lives as if God does not exist. Psalm 14:1 A fool has no faith in the existence of God and does not subscribe to His Laws because he doesn't believe He exists. He sees those who do as fools because he can't understand why they would follow God.

The Bible's definition of foolishness is, however, more restrictive. It says in Ephesians 5:17, "Therefore do not be foolish, but understand what the Lord's will is." So, the basic difference is that a fool refuses to acknowledge God's existence, while the foolish fails to acknowledge the enormity of God's power to intervene in our lives.

The reason we must seek God's will is to know what God wants for us in every situation, which represents His best for us, and by thanking God in everything, we open our hearts and lives to God for His intervention. Psalm 50:23 states, "Whoever offers praise glorifies Me; And to him who orders his conduct aright I will show the salvation of God." God wants us to receive His life, and as a thanksgiver, you are guaranteed a divine intervention of the positive kind.

Apostle Paul was a major proponent of thanksgiving who also modelled the principle and demonstrated what could be achieved by giving thanks to God in everything. God that led Paul and his Apostolic team to the City of Philippi, where they were attacked and unjustly incarcerated for preaching the Gospel in the power of God.

However, because they understood the principle of giving thanks in everything, instead of griping about the injustice of their circumstances, they initiated a thanksgiving service in their dungeon. We all know how things turned out; God came visiting and busted them out of prison. He ultimately transformed their impromptu Thanksgiving service into a Church plant because He saved the jailer's family and probably some of the inmates.

Thanksgiving as a principle applies to all areas of life. Paul and Silas' response to their trouble did not seem right, but it produced the right outcome. That is how we, too, should approach our difficulties. Thanking God may not seem right, but how best can we prove that Jesus is the same yesterday, today, and forever? Since He has done it before, He will do it again and specifically for us. Hence, you can be thankful for your troubled marriage, tanking business, rebellious children, and any other kind of situation that defies the will of God for your life. After all, everything means everything. A thankful heart attracts God's virtue for breakthroughs that also nullify the devil's attempts to hijack our destiny.

The Bible's injunction to give thanks in everything is not just a suggestion that we may choose to disregard or obey as a matter of convenience, but a commandment we must obey. It is you saying, 'God, whatever my situation, I am committed to being thankful, even when I face challenges and negativities.' Doing that is understandably difficult, but God assures us that this is His will for us because doing so keeps us in the right mindset that stops us from doing something foolish.

5. Fifth, **through thanksgiving, God blocks the path that leads to satanic entrapment that you should not have been traveling and keeps you on the right path.**

The Bible says that God anoints your head with the oil of joy, and your cup overflows. Psalm 23:5 An epidemic of depression is sweeping through the world and is particularly severe in the first-world countries. Japan suffers from the highest annual rate of suicides, closely followed by the Scandinavian countries, which have long periods of darkness. Interestingly, these places have material and financial wealth and everything that those in the developing world aspire to, thinking, 'If only we could have what they have.' But why then do they kill themselves? Why are they depressed?

This proves that materialism can only make you happy up to a point; it confers comfort but does not give joy. Countries where people are materially poor, surprisingly, rank higher on the happiness scale. They are happy because they have understood and mastered the principle of giving thanks in everything. They may not have much, but they are joyful and content with the little they have.

I read a story involving a wealthy man who saw a group of manual labourers playing with each other by the roadside. Entranced by their carefree attitude and joy, he ordered his driver to stop the car as he watched these relatively poor people enjoying themselves, something he had lost the ability to do due to the cares of his wealth.

Some of us have allowed the cares of life to steal our joy. The Bible says that God has anointed us with oil of gladness, so that He can lift away from us the spirit of heaviness or depression, proving that God does not want us to be depressed. That's why the Bible says in Proverbs 17:22 that "A joyful heart is good medicine, but a broken spirit dries up the bones." Being joyful positively impacts your health.

Someone I know went for a therapy session after suffering from bouts of depression. When I examined some of the suggestions they were asked to follow, I started laughing. They might as well have lifted them from the Bible. They suggested thinking positive thoughts. If only they had searched the Scriptures, they would have realised that God was already there.

Thinking good things or positive thoughts was also Apostle Paul's suggestion in Philippians 4:8 He said, "Finally, brethren, whatever things are true, whatever things are noble, whatever things are just, whatever things are pure, whatever things are lovely, whatever things are of good report, if there is any virtue and if there is anything praiseworthy—meditate on these things."

Thanksgiving channels you towards positive thoughts because you know His thoughts and plan for you are thoughts of good and not of evil. You are therefore expectant of experiencing the goodness of God.

So, when faced with a deathly situation, you declare, 'I shall not die, but live to declare the works of God.' Psalm 118:17 With that kind of attitude exuding positivity, how can you be depressed?

So, thanksgiving stops you from getting depressed. I know that there are different causes and manifestations of depression. It can be medically induced or result from stress. Depression can also be due to hormonal imbalance, or it can have spiritual underpinnings.

Regardless of the source or cause, understand that God has power over all forms of depression, for if we don't believe that the spiritual realm has power over the physical, then why are we praying? We pray and expect that something will happen, and it does. So, when we thank God, we are asking God to take control of our lives so that His glory can be seen in us. Hence, rather than becoming victims of your circumstances, through thanksgiving, you defy and master your situation in the power of God and become the master of your own destiny.

This is why, for example, Prophet Habakkuk could declare in Habakkuk 3:17-19 that, 'Though the fig tree does not blossom and there are no cattle in the store ...' He said, 'Yet I will praise God.' Although his circumstances looked bleak, Habakkuk was determined not to allow them to dictate his destiny. He would not allow what people were saying or doing, or what they thought, to distract him from the victory that is his in God. So, even in difficult circumstances, you can still thank God because you know that God is in control of your life.

6. Sixth, **understand that thanksgiving is always the right prayer for all times.** The Bible enjoins us to pray with all kinds of prayer, and one of those prayers is thanksgiving. By thanking God, you can never go wrong because you are guaranteed to pray the will of God.

Just praying, 'God, I bless your holy name. I worship you,' can in the least make you feel good, but at most make God feel even better about you because you are prioritising pleasing Him in your distress, regardless of your discomfort, and that secures His respect and positive response.

So, when the Bible says 'In everything give thanks', it is saying that you can never go wrong by thanking God. So, if you don't want to fail, thanksgiving is what you should do. If you want God to work for you and fight your battles, thanksgiving is your ultimate prayer to enlist His help. It is the best prayer in the world because you can never pray amiss or go wrong. Thanksgiving is like praying the Holy Ghost; you can never pray amiss because you are always praying the perfect will of God.

7. Seven, **Satan always seeks to derail us with his attacks. Thanksgiving empowers us to stay on track, avoid derailment, discover God's will, and frustrate the devil in his job, which is to steal, kill, and destroy.** Your job is to ensure that you enjoy God's

abundance, and thanksgiving is how you accomplish that. Whatever it is that the enemy is trying to do, because you are thanking God, you're putting yourself under God's will and authority, and can therefore resist the devil. You are saying to the devil, 'I defy whatever evil you are planning concerning me.' Thanksgiving is God's will, and its fruit is life abundant.

8. Eighth, **when our faith is tested, thanksgiving ensures that we are not tested to destruction as Satan intended but refined by God for progress unto better things.** Understand that there will be a trial of your faith. So, if you say I have faith, as we all do, know that your faith will one day be tested to certify its genuineness. However, even when your faith is being tested, because you understand what it means to thank God, you are still able to maintain a positive mindset and perspective about what God is doing. That stops your faith from disintegrating and spurs it to successfully go through the refining fire of trials to fulfil your destiny.

9. Ninth, **thanksgiving protects you from the worst of the impact of your circumstances by building your hope up for the best that is available in Christ.** I have previously shared that when I was going through what was then the worst situation in my life, I did not feel its full impact because I was focused on and could thus only see the best that God has in mind for me. The reason is that Satan failed to distract me. He could not restrict or falsify my perspectives to only see the bad things that were happening to me, and not the improvements God was

actively making to my life through the difficult experience. Thanksgiving meant that I was not playing the devil's game and allowing God to play the enemy at his own game and defeat him for my benefit.

The reason many give up is because they conclude that life is not worth living. They have no hope or a reason to live. David questioned himself about his depression and supplied the answer by referencing hope. He asked, Psalm 42:5, "Why are you cast down, O my soul? And why are you disquieted within me? Hope in God, for I shall yet praise Him for the help of His countenance." So, yes, things can be difficult, but God is faithful. He will always come through for us.

10. Tenth, **thanksgiving douses any sense of entitlement we may have and enables us to genuinely count our blessings and be more appreciative of God's goodness.**

Why do you feel that something bad can't happen to you? It is because some of us have gotten to the stage where we feel as if God owes us and must compensate us? We develop a sense of entitlement that expects God to serve our interests regardless of His will for us. Even when things unexpectedly happen to us, instead of humbling ourselves in His presence, we challenge and accuse God of incompetence because we feel that God has not protected us as He should have.

What about the things that God has done? If you start thanking God and start reflecting on the things God has done for you, you will quickly realise that focusing on God's previous deeds will stir up hope in you for present and future blessings.

The Bible says to give thanks, but it doesn't say that you must feel thankful to do so. It is about principle and not emotion. As you execute the principle, your emotions will follow. So, just thank God even if you don't feel like it. You do it regardless of how you feel because it is the will of God for you in Christ Jesus, and I'm sure that all of us want to do the will of God.

Thanksgiving is a matter of obedience, and the best and proven way to ensure that you obey God's word and fulfil His will for your life is to give thanks in everything.

3

Thanksgiving: Nurturing Your Seed Of Greatness

"Be anxious for nothing, but in everything by prayer and supplication, with thanksgiving, let your requests be made known to God; and the peace of God, which surpasses all understanding, will guard your hearts and minds through Christ Jesus." Philippians 4:6-7

Having tackled why thanksgiving is important and how it helps us maintain our stand in the will of God. We will now tackle the subject from a different perspective, looking at thanksgiving as a seed. A seed is what you sow to obtain a harvest. So, if you intend to have a harvest, you must first sow a seed.

As discussed in the previous chapter, thanksgiving operates in three distinct but interconnected forms: anticipatory, reflectory, and celebratory. But how do you translate either anticipatory or reflectory thanksgiving, which represents the staging points of our victory, into the celebratory thanksgiving that celebrates our triumphs?

I remember jubilantly announcing to my Pastor that I had found my life's mission. I had been observing an extended time of praying and fasting, seeking an answer to one question, 'Lord God, what would you have me do?'

After seeking God for months, wanting to know His will for my life, God finally revealed what He wanted me to do. He said, 'I have called you to a life of praise and worship. With later clarification, I understood that God has called me to make victors of victims and build a people of praise for His end-time move.

I excitedly rushed to my Pastor to share the good news. I said, I believe God is telling me to concentrate on the area of praise and worship. Other than leading worship in Church, I did not even know too much about the subject and was looking forward to learning more about praise and worship to fulfil my calling.

The first question my Pastor asked was, 'Are you sure you're not one of those who praise God in everything?' I was taken aback by the direct line of questioning, but I understood the reticence.

One of the first books I read on praise several years earlier was Merlin Carothers's 'From prison to praise'. He had explored the subject from the perspective of praising God in everything, and the question that was raised in people's minds is, should you praise God even when bad things happen to you?

My pastor's singular question sowed a seed in my mind that became a quest, and after many years of studying and practising praise and worship, I believe that I can give a true and biblical response to that question. For 30 years, I've been researching and trying to understand why it is that we should give thanks to God in everything. I have also explored different approaches that also work.

For example, in my three-volume work on praise and worship, titled **'The Praise Revolution Is Now!'**, I explored the genesis of praise and worship and as a covenant that obliges God to respond to our praise with His blessings according to His word, Exodus 23:25-27, and Numbers 10:9-10. I also looked at the role of praise and worship will play in the end time move of God.

However, a different and equally valid approach to answering that question, 'Should you praise God or give thanks in everything as Scriptures have said?' is to understand and see thanksgiving as a seed you sow in whatever circumstances you find yourself. You can then understand, as dictated by natural and supernatural laws, that although you sowed your seed initially under duress in the throes of your trouble, Scripture guarantees that there will come a time when you shall reap a harvest in joy that leads to more celebratory thanksgiving.

So, how do we know that thanksgiving is a seed? Philippians 4:6 says, "Be anxious for nothing, but in everything, with prayer, supplication, and thanksgiving, make your request known to God.' So, if your question is, 'But you have only just finished asking, why are you also thanking God? Why does God require us to thank Him when we have yet to receive physical proof of answers to our prayers?'

God's instruction to us is, 'Be anxious for nothing, but in everything with prayer, supplication, and thanksgiving, make your request known, making thanksgiving an intrinsic part of our prayer. Therefore, we do not have to wait until God has done it before thanking Him, because our thanksgiving is by faith. In anticipation of God's move, we call things which are not, as though they were. Hence, the import of God's word to us is "When you've just finished praying by faith, start thanking me in anticipation of my blessing."

This means that God always intended the thanksgiving insert in prayer to be like a seed sown in anticipation of a future harvest. Therefore, a seed is not something you consume, but an investment you sow, regardless of circumstances, in expectation of a greater future reward. So, during your initial prayer, God's expectation is not for you to reap an immediate harvest, but to sow your thanksgiving by faith, trusting in God for a future harvest.

To comprehensively address the issue of the correct placement of thanksgiving in prayer, we will examine the subject from the perspective of the interaction of natural and supernatural Laws, as we examine the four Laws of Harvest, the Law of Process, and the Law of Sacrifice.

The first Law of harvest states that if you don't sow, you can't reap. The second Law states that if you sow a single seed, you reap a multiple of what you have sown. The third Law states that if you sow one kind or species, you reap the same. The fourth Law addresses the issue of sacrifice. If you go out to sow with weeping, you shall reap in joy. Why? Because it shows that the nature of your seed is changing. The seed you sowed at the beginning in anticipation, when you were crying and saying, 'Lord, I don't feel like praising you right now because I need this thing, but I will still praise and exalt you regardless of how I feel.' That is your seed of thanksgiving. It is destined to transform into a harvest of joy. That is the Law of Sacrifice.

You sacrifice something to a higher power by giving up something precious to you. The Law of Sacrifice states that you must give up something to go up in life.

We all could have stopped our education at secondary school, taken up jobs, and started earning money, but most of us chose not to. We delayed our craving for immediate gratification to gain more qualifications, whether a first degree, second, or third, along with professional credentials that would enable us to earn more money later. We all agree that such a sacrifice was worthwhile. That is the Law of Sacrifice.

As parents, many of us gladly make sacrifices for our children. When you could have gone for the latest cars, you instead used that money to get your children the best education you can afford because you want to put them on the best pedestal from which to start their journey in life. Rather than buy the newest car, you bought a ten-year-old car and just about managed it. That is a sacrifice. You are trusting that you will reap a harvest in the future. That is exactly what we are doing whenever we thank God in expectation of answered prayers – making a sacrifice of thanksgiving.

So, let me state for the record, the four Laws of harvest are:

1. The first Law of harvest states that a seed will always produce multiple what is sown. "Most assuredly, I say to you, unless a grain of wheat falls into the ground and dies, it remains alone; but if it dies, it produces much grain." John 12:24 This means that if you treat thanksgiving as a seed, then you can expect that when you sow that seed in times of need or difficult

circumstances by praising and exalting God, you will reap a harvest. As you sow and nurture that seed, it will grow and produce a harvest. That is the first Law of harvest - sow one, reap a multiple.

2. The second Law of harvest states that a seed will always produce after its kind. Galatians 6:7 states, "Do not be deceived, God is not mocked; for whatever a man sows, that he will also reap." Sow orange and reap more oranges.

3. The third Law of harvest states that "While the earth remains, Seedtime and harvest, Cold and heat, Winter and summer, And day and night Shall not cease." Genesis 8:22 Although man has been able to manipulate the growing seasons of some plants, the fact that we must sow to reap has not changed. It is about timing and regularity. There will always be a time to sow and a time to reap. This is where the Law of Process comes into play. For example, even when God has said to a woman, 'You shall have a child', He still doesn't break the Law process. The woman must gestate the baby for 9 months before birthing it. The Law of Process states that even when God has promised you something, there's always a processing time to gestate it. It won't suddenly appear; it must wait for its appointed time. As you give thanks to God, the Law of process kicks in. You may not be able to see it but understand that God will fulfil His word concerning you, because it is a principle.

4. The fourth Law of harvest is as stated in Psalm 126:5-6: "Those who sow in tears shall reap in joy. He who continually goes forth weeping, bearing

seed for sowing, shall doubtless come again with rejoicing, bringing his sheaves with him." So, the moment you start thanking God sacrificially, you are setting the Law of process in motion by faith, and saying, 'Lord God, because I trust you, and believe your word concerning me, I know that I may be sowing my seed in tears, but I am confident that the time is coming when I shall rejoice before you and reap a harvest of joy.

Understanding that thanksgiving is a seed means that we all have a choice to either sow our seed, which qualifies us for a harvest of grace, or refuse to sow it and thus reap nothing or worse. Whatever your circumstances, you cannot say to God, 'God, I don't have a seed to sow.' Where thanksgiving is concerned, you will always have a seed to sow, because it is right there in your mouth. Apostle Paul's prayer in 2 Corinthians 9:10 is that "Now may He who supplies seed to the sower, and bread for food, supply and multiply the seed you have sown and increase the fruits of your righteousness."

God's provision of the seed to sow is by default. You don't need to stress yourself to find it. It's already within you. Just do it and set the Law of process in motion to work for you. Hence, His directive that we should be anxious for nothing, but in everything with prayer, supplication, and sowing the seed of thanksgiving, make your request known to God. Hence, understand that:

1. We all have a seed of thanksgiving to sow; we just must decide whether we will sow it or not. We can choose to start sowing the seed we have to hand or grumble that 'God, you didn't do this or that. You are wasting your time because God cannot process the seed of thanksgiving that you have not sown. Satan will be the one processing your seed of complaint,

and you are giving him more ammunition with which to hurt you. God is a good farmer, and we should be like Him. We should sow our seed in sacrifice because sowing can come with a cost. Psalm 126:6 says whoever goes out with his seed crying because he wants to eat it, but still says, 'God, I will exalt you', will come back with a harvest of joy.

2. God has hidden the seed of thanksgiving in every situation that you find yourself. We have a saying that even in adversity, God always makes room for thanksgiving. You then realise that things could have been worse than they are. You may need to dig deep within to search for that seed, and once you find it, you leverage it in your prayers to activate your covenant with God to manifest His guaranteed greater harvest.

3. Thanksgiving obeys the Law of faith. Thanking God in difficult situations in expectation of divine intervention requires taking a step of faith, and nothing moves God more than you deciding to trust God by sowing your seed of thanksgiving. So, you must first sow your seed before it can grow and produce the harvest you are actively expecting. This means that you must be intentional in your thanksgiving. Being intentional means that you say to God, 'I know that things are tough, but I have decided to praise you, regardless of my circumstances.'

By being intentional with your thanksgiving, you are saying to God, 'God, I know the seed of thanksgiving exists in me. You shall turn it into a harvest of joy.' And that's exactly what God will do. Also, understand that being intentional means that you don't just sow your seed of thanksgiving and abandon it. No good farmer does that. Instead, he cultivates and protects his seed to maximise its productivity. It must be the same with us.

Some would thank God one moment, saying, 'Lord, I bless you', and then complain the next. Being intentional requires consistency in your thanksgiving. Sometimes you have to say, "Lord God, I am intentionally cultivating my seed of thanksgiving as I praise and exalt you.' and mean it. For some situations, you only need to bless God for a few minutes, and the harvest manifests immediately. For some, it takes a few hours. For some, a few months, and for some, years.

So long as you nurture your seed and do everything to bring the process to completion, it doesn't matter how long it takes. God, who gives seed to the sower and bread to the eater, will cause your harvest to come in the fullness of time. So, your thanksgiving must be intentional, for whatever you sow is also what you will reap. God has guaranteed that as you sow in righteousness, you will reap in mercy. Hosea 10:12

So, we see all these Laws of nature coming into play one way or the other. When you understand these laws that what you sow is what you reap, then you know that the power of life and death are in the tongue, and those who love it will eat its fruit, and understanding that fact means that you know that as you thank and exalt Him, God will come through for you.

4. With thanksgiving, you start by anticipating but always end with celebrating. God answers some prayers immediately, and you go straight to celebration, but most times, when God doesn't answer immediately, you have no physical proof that God has done it, but you know in your heart that God has done it. So, you wait in an attitude of anticipatory thanksgiving until your physical proof manifests, enabling you to show it to the world and say, "Hey, this is what God has done."

So, say, 'God, because I know that you're going to do it, I just want to exalt you.' So, you praise God and thank Him in anticipation of what He will do. The Bible says that Abraham called things which are not as though they were because he was anticipating that they would be. That is the Law of faith. You too must call things as you want them to be, even when they are not, because you know that they shall be. Why? Because what you say is what you get.

The Bible says that 'The power of life and death are in the tongue', Proverbs 18:21 and that 'The words that I speak, they are spirit and they are life.' John 6:63 This makes it difficult for you to thank God and complain at the same time. You can't genuinely thank God and also say negative things at the same time. Why? Because thanking God causes your faith to rise. That was what Abraham did. He started with praise by saying, 'Thank you, Lord. I bless you because I am the father of many nations. Thank you, Lord, for you have changed my name. I know my life will reflect your glory.' The Bible says that his faith grew strong as he gave praise to God. Romans 4:20 The more you thank God, the more you have reason to thank Him, because you start believing in your heart, for with the heart man believes, and with the mouth confession is made unto salvation. Romans 10:10

5. Understand that your thanksgiving is the only seed you have to sow, and as you keep sowing and nurturing it, one day, something good will happen. That was what happened to Abraham.

For a long time, I thought that Abraham had to praise God for 17 years as he awaited the manifestation of the promise in Isaac. Well, I was wrong. Abraham only praised God intensely for 3 months before his wife became pregnant. Once he believed God's word and started praising God, the Bible says that his faith grew so strong that he entertained no doubt whatsoever about God's ability to fulfil His promise. So, Abraham's thanksgiving and praise crowded out every doubt he may have had, pushing him beyond the point of no return and certainty that God would do as He had promised. From his perspective, the surprise would have been if God had not done it. We, too, need to get to that point, and thanksgiving is how we can get there.

So, you often start with anticipatory thanksgiving by saying, 'God, I bless you because you are perfecting your work in me, knowing that whatever you have begun, you always finish.' Whatever starts with thanksgiving always ends with thanksgiving. The only change is the nature of the thanksgiving. You start with anticipation, saying, "God will do it", and finish by saying, "God has done it."

6. Finally, your harvest of thanksgiving is always in multiple dimensions to what you sowed, and that is the reason your joy will increase. Ecclesiastes 11:1 states, "Cast your bread upon the waters, for you will find it after many days." What you find will be the multiple of what you sowed. The Bible says, 'Until now you have asked nothing in My name. Ask, and you will receive, that your joy may be full.' John 16:24

God understands that although the Bible exhorts us to rejoice always, sometimes we must compel ourselves to do it. There is a difference between pushing ourselves to rejoice and our joy overflowing naturally. The latter happens effortlessly, like water gushing out of a faucet, because it is celebratory, whereas the other is more like sitting still in anticipation. We must dig deep to get to the water source.

So, when the Bible says that we should sow our seed in expectation of a multiple harvest, the same principle applies to our joy. So long as you are faithful to do it, regardless of your circumstances or how you feel about it, you can expect a result. God's promise to us is that 'Though weeping endures a night, joy comes in the morning. Your joy overflowing will come.

The dawning of a new morning implies that you live in hope. It is the reason you know that you cannot die just yet, because God must fulfil His promise of joy to you. This realisation was the reason David proclaimed, 'I shall not die. I shall live to declare the works of God.' Psalm 118:17 Why? Because he knew that he wasn't going anywhere yet, with God's promise unfulfilled. He knew that God would not allow you to die before He could fulfil His word to you.

Hence, understand that living in anticipation of the fulfilment of God's promise means that God is committed to preserving your life. His word shall come to pass in the fullness of time because 'In His time, He makes all things beautiful.' Ecclesiastes 3:11

So, in whatever situation we find ourselves, and whatever the circumstances, even when you don't feel like it, give thanks to God. It always works. And if you have been thanking God in anticipation for a while and have yet to experience your breakthrough, continue to thank God and persevere to the end, because His word can never fail.

For those of us who we are reflecting on the grace of God and see the reason to be thankful for how far God has brought us, we can do no better than to continue, for in doing so, we are positioning ourselves to receive more of God's grace for greater exploit. So, continue on your thankful path, for more of God awaits you.

If you would like to sow your seed of thanksgiving and thus commence your journey to reaping a greater harvest of joy, this is a good time to start, first by thanking God for your salvation, for being alive, and the hope that is in Jesus Christ.

Say, 'Lord God, I thank you for the opportunity that I have today to hear your word. Help me to be thankful so that I can worship you in spirit and in truth.'

Thankfully, we all have a reason to thank God and exalt His name because His seed of thanksgiving exists in all of us, sometimes growing healthily as we thank God, or lying dormant because we have not yet stirred it to life with our thanksgiving.

Let us activate our seeds of thanksgiving by telling God, 'Lord God, today, I am being intentional in sowing my seed of thanksgiving to you. Cause the fruit of my lips to bring praise to you. The words of thanksgiving shall ensue from my mouth and glorify your name.'

'Father, I thank you, for the Bible says, 'Be anxious for nothing, but in everything with prayer, supplication, and thanksgiving, make your request known to God. I declare no more worries, for I shall praise you because I know you have done it. I exalt you because you shall cause my joy to be full.'

'My joy may presently be constrained, but because the joy of the Lord is my strength, I receive strength from you. Lord God, fill me up with your joy overflowing, so that I can come before you rejoicing, bringing in the sheaves of harvest for your glory.'

4

Weaponising Your Thanksgiving: How To Transform The Ordinary Into The Extraordinary

"In everything give thanks, for this is the will of God for you in Christ Jesus." 1 Thessalonians 5:18 Ephesians 5:20 states, "Giving thanks always for all things to God the Father in the name of our Lord Jesus Christ", and that can be a bit difficult for us to understand.

It's easy enough for us to give thanks in good times, but very difficult to thank God for difficult times. Yet, the Bible says, 'In and for everything'.

The reason the Bible commands us to give thanks in and for everything is that God is directing us to turn ordinary thanksgiving into a weapon of war with which we fight spiritual battles and attract God's presence, because God inhabits the praises of His people. Psalm 22:3

So, when you give thanks, you are inviting God into your life and acknowledging the fact that God is the one in control of your life.

Let's start by trying to understand what it is to weaponise something. The word 'Weaponise' means to turn into a weapon. A microphone is ordinarily a means of amplifying words to effect communication with a larger audience. However, if I become angry and use the same microphone to hit somebody on the head, it is no longer being used for the primary purpose it was designed for and has become a weapon, thanks to the new use you are putting it to.

Hence, to weaponise means to modify or adapt for use as a weapon of war something ordinary or something not originally designed as a weapon. It is to change the use of something to harm or kill.

Anything can conceivably be weaponised, however benign. All that needs to change is the motivation behind the use. A car ordinarily designed to transport you from A – B can be transformed into a weapon of death in the hands of a maniac or someone motivated to cause harm because you have transformed something ordinary into a means of achieving a goal.

Now that we know what it entails to weaponise something, the next question is who weaponises? Well, God does. The devil does, too, and so do you. Anyone can weaponise anything. We have all taken something ordinary and transformed it into something that can help or harm somebody else. That is weaponisation.

Sometimes, it is our words. Many people have been scarred for life by the careless or deliberate words of others, and many have been helped by affirming words. Those who engage in spiritual warfare understand that words are prime weapons, and even the Bible acknowledges that the power of life and death are in the tongue. Proverbs 18:21 Hence, those who say that sticks and stones may break my bones, but words cannot harm me, are either naïve or being untruthful, for our words are very powerful. Whenever somebody uses your weakness against you, they are weaponising your attribute to destroy you.

God also weaponises. He can weaponise people or things to fulfil His purpose. For example, when Joshua commanded the sun to stay still so that he could defeat his enemies, God complemented his effort by raining hailstones from heaven on those who were hiding from Joshua and killed them. God weaponised Joshua and charged him to fulfil His purpose. He also weaponised hailstones for the same purpose. Joshua 10:11

God weaponised Prophet Jeremiah, by declaring in Jeremiah 51:20-26, "You are my battle axe and my weapons of warfare." The implication for us is that God is saying, 'I am weaponising you as an instrument of war to use you to fulfil my purpose. Yes, you are a human being, but you are also a weapon in God's hand, charged to operate in His power and fulfil His purpose. You are no longer ordinary!

The sooner you understand that you are God's weapons, the quicker you will commit to fulfilling God's agenda for your life. God recognises that you are human, but He has chosen to weaponise you to fulfil His purpose. Joel 3:10 enjoins us to 'Beat your plowshares into swords And your pruning hooks into spears; Let the weak say, 'I am strong.'

In ancient times, when countries seldom had a professional or standing army, it fell to the citizens to fight and defend themselves from their enemies. There were not many weapons to go around in times of war. There were armouries, but an insufficient number of weapons. Hence, it was a case of bring-your-own armour. Whenever trouble flares up, ordinary farmers would rush to the blacksmith to convert their ordinary iron farming implements into weapons of war. They turn their ploughs into swords and other offensive and defensive weapons for use in battles for survival.

They are weaponising their metal implements by turning them from benign use into lethal weapons. They were turning the plowshares they used to cultivate food to feed themselves into weapons to fight their enemies and stay alive. God is also calling us to do the same thing.

Whoever you are, and whatever you do, God expects you to turn whatever you use to feed yourself into the means of fighting spiritual warfare and doing ministry. Whether you are a doctor or a teacher, in the hands of God, your profession becomes an avenue for you to preach the gospel, thereby turning something ordinary into a deadly weapon.

So, God weaponises, and so does the devil, for you are subject to do the bidding of whoever controls you. People weaponise too. The phenomenon of suicide bombers and assassins, whereby people turn other people into weapons for their own ends or in the service of the state, is nothing new. It is one thing to turn a man into a weapon by training him to use weapons to kill, and a whole different level to make the man a weapon on his own, whereby survival of the attack is optional. Some people opt for that kind of 'glorious' end and pay the ultimate price for their cause.

Some turn themselves into suicide bombers for religious, political or personal reasons. They wear a bomb vest that detonates and kills themselves and other people. That's one way of weaponising a human being for a cause.

Fictional characters such as James Bond of the British Secret Service, MI6, and Jason Bourne of the CIA were trained to be killing machines who usually manage to survive to fight another day in the service of their countries.

After God weaponising mankind, and man weaponising man, the next level in the weaponisation spectrum is man weaponising other things, such as entities, processes, or behaviours. Weaponising our thanksgiving falls into this category, even though it also incorporates the previous categories of God weaponising us as His battle axe.

Another dimension in our understanding of how we weaponise our thanksgiving is to understand that we are God's primary weapon. This implies that not all weapons are the same, or used for the same purpose, although usually to accomplish the same end of victory. In spiritual warfare, there are primary, secondary, and even tertiary weapons.

The understanding is that the utility and efficacy of one level of weapon build on and determine the efficacy of the other higher forms from the bottom up. So, a deficiency in a primary weapon negatively impacts the efficiency of the secondary and tertiary weapons and can sometimes render them useless.

As God's primary weapon, God says, "In my hands I can use you to do anything." This makes you a significant spoke in the wheel of God's battle plan. Everything else radiates from you, either positively or otherwise. God cannot fight His battles without you, especially as it pertains to you. Apostle Paul echoed this sentiment by saying 'I can do all things through Christ who strengthens me.' So, whenever God wants to fight a battle or achieve an important objective, He turns to mankind, that is, you and me, and deploys us in battle. However, before He lets us loose in battle, He trains us. David alluded to this fact by saying that God trains his hands for war and his fingers to fight. Psalm 144:1 It is only as God is satisfied with us that He deploys us to obtain victory in His name.

The next stage in our understanding of the weaponisation of our thanksgiving is that God never sends us into battle empty-handed; that would be inconsiderate of Him and suicidal of us. He gives us weapons to fight with, although our enemies might beg to differ and argue that they are no weapons at all. Whatever its deficiency, we know that God always gives us something to fight with, and to the consternation of our enemies, delivers victory to us. Usually, the goal of His under equipment is to teach us to trust in Him and not in our weapons. Again, David resonated this fact by saying, "Some trust in chariots, and some in horses; But we will remember the name of the Lord our God." Psalm 20:7

An example of the kind of weapon God can place in our hands to fight our enemies is the jawbone of an ass that Samson used to kill a thousand Philistines in battle. Samson was caught in a Philistine ambush without any recognisable weapon with which to fight his enemies. He happened to see the jawbone of an ass lying around, an ordinary and useless thing, but which, in the power of God, became an instrument of death to the Philistines. By the time God and

Samson were finished, a thousand Philistines lay dead. Samson was God's primary weapon, and the jawbone became his secondary weapon. So, whatever God gives you to fight the enemy with constitutes your secondary weapon. You remain His primary weapon.

It was the same with David several generations later. David wanted to face Goliath, who came heavily armed and bristling with iron weapons and a coat of mail. All David had was a sling and five stones. Most Israelites saw David's token effort as a desperate suicide mission to save face, since everybody knew that a sling and a stone could not harm somebody wearing protective armour.

David begged to differ and chose to bet his life on the fact that he knew that he was God's primary weapon. He understood that Goliath stood no chance against him. So, he declared, "You have come against me with sword and spear, but I come against you in the name of the Lord of hosts." Then he used his stone and slung it at Goliath, and because God was guiding it, two things happened.

God directed the stone to the weakest part of Goliath's armour, and then, when the stone was in flight, God did something else: He significantly increased the speed of the stone and transformed it from a dangerous stone to a lethal bullet. So, what proof do I have that God turned the stone into a bullet? Well, if somebody were to throw a stone at you, depending on how close they are to you, and hence the speed of travel and inherent power, the worst you may suffer is a bump on your head, with the attendant headache. In the extreme, you will suffer a concussion, which may or may not be fatal. The stone will not penetrate your skull, as it did Goliath's, because it lacks the sufficient speed and power to cause that level of havoc.

A bullet discharged from a gun travel at over five times the speed of a stone shot from a sling, and that is the reason for the penetrative power of a bullet. Goliath never saw it coming and probably never felt its impact. He just slumped and died, and all that was left for David to do was cut off his head as a trophy of battle.

The power of God propelled that stone, guided it, and speeded it up so that by the time it reached Goliath, it had become unstoppable and lethal. The weapon (sling and stone) worked only because David knew who he was – God's battle axe. Hence, the only way that the weapons you have will work for you is when you know that you have God behind you. It is also the reason you can be confident that no weapon forged against you shall prosper. Isaiah 54:17 The God who has given us victory and has won the battle for us will ensure that our enemies' weapons fail to work against us.

The important question we need to ask is What weapons has God given to us? In 2 Corinthians 10:4, the Bible says, 'The weapons of our warfare are not carnal.' They are not fleshy because our battles are seldom solely physical. However, they are spiritual and mighty through God for the pulling down of strongholds, casting down imaginations, and bringing into subjection every high thing that exalts itself against the knowledge of God.

So, the purpose of whatever weapon God has given to you is to fight spiritual warfare and win in the power of God. So, what are these weapons?

Ephesians 6:10-18 provides a comprehensive list:

"Finally, my brethren, be strong in the Lord and in the power of His might. Put on the whole armour of God, that you may be able to stand against the wiles of the devil. For we do not wrestle against flesh and blood, but against principalities, against powers, against the rulers of the darkness of this age, against spiritual hosts of wickedness in the heavenly places. Therefore take up the whole armour of God, that you may be able to withstand in the evil day, and having done all, to stand. Stand therefore, having girded *your waist with truth, having put on the breastplate of righteousness, and having shod your feet with the preparation of the gospel of peace; above all, taking the shield of faith with which you will be able to quench all the fiery darts of the wicked one. And take the helmet of salvation, and the sword of the Spirit*, which is the word of God; **praying always with all prayer and supplication in the Spirit**, being watchful to this end with all perseverance and supplication for all the saints—" (*Emphasis mine*)

So, our spiritual weapons consist of the belt of truth, breastplate of righteousness, gospel of peace, shield of faith, helmet of salvation, and sword of the Spirit. These are both offensive and defensive weapons, and with them, we are dressed to kill.

Let us take the word of God, the sword of the Spirit, as an example. It is primarily an offensive weapon but can also serve a defensive purpose when required. Whenever you wield a sword in offence, you're going after somebody else. However, even primarily defensive weapons like a shield do more than defend. Apart from protecting you from the darts of the enemy, in desperate situations, our shields can serve an offensive purpose. In close-quarters battles, you can use it to swat your enemy aside as you attack him with your sword.

However, note that apart from the obvious weapons mentioned above, prayer is also mentioned, but not alongside the others. Why is that? Why do we need to pray all kinds of prayers in spiritual warfare? It is because prayer serves as our weapon delivery system. Having weapons is not enough to win battles. Even being trained to use weapons does not guarantee victory in battles if you cannot make your weapons count on the battlefield. Prayer is how we work our spiritual weapons and make them count on the battlefield.

Interestingly, Apostle Paul alluded to different kinds of prayer, implying that not all kinds of prayer achieve the same thing. Effectual prayer requires praying the right kind of prayer for the right situation. Hence, it is not enough to pray; you must also pray the right prayer to guarantee victory. Prayer is what launches your weapon at the enemy and elicits God's help to defeat him. Without the agency of effectual prayer, our weapons are rendered ineffectual, and the enemy wins.

So, what kinds of prayer can we pray and in what circumstances? Below are a list of 5 kinds of prayer and their corresponding circumstances. This list is neither exhaustive nor intended as an in-depth definition of the different kinds of prayer. They are listed to show how the kind of prayer we pray affects its effectuality:

1. **Prayer of agreement**: usually required when you need more than one person to pray. It multiplies spiritual firepower, aids effectuality, and

elevates prayer to the level of geometric progression where one shall chase a thousand, and two, ten thousand. Deuteronomy 32:30 Jesus Christ said in Matthew 18:19, "Again I say to you that if two of you agree on earth concerning anything that they ask, it will be done for them by My Father in heaven."

2. **Prayer of faith**: "And the prayer of faith will save the sick, and the Lord will raise him up. And if he has committed sins, he will be forgiven." James 5:15

3. **Prayer of intercession**: To intercede means to plead on behalf or to stand in the gap. It is prayer that focuses on people or situations other than us, pleading for divine intervention, Job 22:30

4. **Prayer of supplication**: To supplicate means to plead for one's needs. So, it is prayer solely focused on God meeting your legitimate needs. God knows that we have needs; it is the reason He counsels that we should not be anxious but should present our needs in prayer as we supplicate, and God will grant our prayers, provided we ask in His name and according to His will. John 14:12-14

5. **Prayer of adoration and thanksgiving**: Praise, worship, and thanksgiving constitute another form of prayer. Its uniqueness is in the fact that it is not only a weapon delivery system, but also a lethal weapon in its own right. So, every time you thank God, you are praying because thanksgiving is prayer. It is the perfect prayer because it is the will of God

for us in Christ Jesus. So, whenever we thank God, we can never pray amiss. Philippians 4:6 says, "Be anxious for nothing, but in everything with prayer, supplication, and thanksgiving make your request known to God."

The Bible commands, 'Don't ever be anxious.' Why do we become anxious? We become anxious when we feel that we cannot control the situation around us. Whenever somebody falls sick around us and we don't know what is going to happen or what we can do, we become anxious. If we are contemplating travelling through a dangerous place, we naturally become anxious.

The way many people deal with anxiety in Western countries is to swallow pills and get hooked on anti-anxiety drugs. When you want to sleep, you just sleep and snore, but some people can only sleep after popping pills because they suffer from anxiety and worry about the intangibles. God says that the best anti-anxiety pill you can ever use is to pray. He commands, 'Do not be anxious, but in everything…'

So, when confronted with a difficult situation, you don't say, 'God, this situation is so big I will reserve it for my anxiety.' God's command, 'In everything,' encompasses both big and small troubles. His solution for tackling any prospective anxiety is prayer.

So, whenever you face challenges that you don't know how to handle, get into your room and start praying. Ask God, 'Father, help me in this situation.' God has promised, 'Call on me and I will answer you. I will show you great and mighty things which you do not know.' Jeremiah 33:3 You can then thank God in anticipation of your breakthrough.

When Hannah prayed, asking God for a son, she had been praying for twenty years, but it seemed as if God was not listening. So, in her frustration, she would pester her husband, "Give me a son." Elkanah's understanding and loving answer was, "Am I not better to you than ten sons?" Hannah's pained reply was, "Obviously not, or I would not be unhappy about my situation. I want a son!"

Then, one day, Hanna went to pray in the temple. As she was praying, she seemed anxious and was seemingly drunk, probably because some who had had too much to drink often sleep off their stupor in the temple to the disdain of the High Priest. Eli thought that Hannah was one of them and confronted her. He said, 'Here we go again. Look at this woman. She's drunk and making a fool of herself.' Hannah's pained response was, 'Sir, I'm not drunk. I am so desperately in need, I have brought my case to God.' Surprised by her clear answer, proving that she indeed was not drunk, Eli had a change of mind and became empathetic to her issue. So, he blessed her and proclaimed that "God has answered your prayers.'

Hannah believed Eli's words and that this was a divine encounter, and the Bible says, 'And she went out, and her countenance changed.' 1 Sam 1:18 Her face, which was always dour, started shining with the light of hope. She knew that she would have a child soon because God had said it.

Her faith meant that Hannah was sure of what she was expecting and certain of what she could not see, and that changed her perspective and impacted her behaviour. She had no reason to remain or be anxious again. Instead, she began actively expecting the manifestation of God's promise to her. The knowledge of God's faithfulness gave Hannah peace, further confirming that her expectations shall not be cut off.

The impact of God's answer to Hannah's prayer that "Do not be anxious, but in everything with prayer, supplication and thanksgiving make your request known to God." was that, "And the peace of God which surpasses all understanding shall keep your hearts and minds through Christ Jesus." proving that the peace of God marshalling our hearts is the title deed of our faith's expectations. Once you have peace about an issue, it means that it is settled, both in heaven and in your heart, and will soon become the reality you live. That was exactly how Hannah felt about her issue of barrenness. She knew that it was no longer a problem. God had resolved it. All she had to do was wait for its manifestation.

Whenever you pray and believe that God has answered you, the proof that you will indeed have God's answer is your peace of mind. That which had been troubling you before will no longer trouble you, because it no longer has any basis to exist in your life. God has handled it. The only thing left for you to do is to thank God in anticipation of His deliverance, hence God's instruction, 'Do not be anxious, but in everything with prayer, supplication and thanksgiving, make your request known to God.'

Ordinarily, you only thank somebody to show appreciation for what they have done for you. It is the proper thing to do. You must show appreciation for a good deed. The major characteristic of anticipatory thanksgiving is that you are thanking God before you have physically seen the answer to your prayers, because you know and trust Him that He will keep His promise and not fail you. Hence, you appreciate God by faith in anticipation of His blessing, confident that He shall do it, because His word is infallible. It is this philosophy that undergirds anticipatory thanksgiving and constitutes your seed of thanksgiving.

Before you can have or become an oak tree of thanksgiving that glorifies God, you must have previously sown and cultivated your acorn of thanksgiving, which qualifies you to expect to reap a harvest of thanksgiving later in adherence to the Laws of harvest.

This leads us to the issue we have been driving at: how to turn your thanksgiving into a weapon. How do you weaponise ordinary things and make them into extraordinary spiritual weapons?

Bearing in mind that anything and anyone can be weaponised, the story of the woman with the issue of blood provides us with an answer and an example of how to either turn yourself into a weapon or weaponise whatever you have. How? She decided to weaponise her encounter with Jesus Christ and make something extraordinary that would benefit and heal her.

Touching Jesus was so commonplace that when He complained, 'Someone touched me', His incredulous disciples could only wonder, 'Master, what is wrong with you?' Have people not been touching you all day? What's so special about now? Jesus' response was to double down and insist, 'I said, somebody touched me.' Why, because it was a special touch, a weaponised touch, the touch of faith. So, faith is how you weaponise anything you have available to conduct spiritual warfare. The things in themselves may be ordinary, but once you confer the power of faith on them, they become extraordinary and can therefore achieve extraordinary things.

Weaponisation is the operative principle behind the practice of Holy Communion, anointing oil, anointed handkerchiefs, mantles, or anything that can convey the power of God to an area of need. It is our means of activating the covenant and power of God to accomplish His will for our lives. It was how Samson transformed the useless jawbone of an ass into a cudgel that killed a thousand Philistines, and enabled David's stone to turn into a bullet that penetrated Goliath's skull and killed him. No wonder Apostle Paul said, 'And faith is your victory'. Faith transforms anything into a weapon.

The woman with the issue of blood weaponised her encounter with Jesus by deciding in her heart that touching the hem of Jesus' garment would elicit the release of her healing anointing. She believed she would receive it and had it and was made whole. Other people milled about and touched Jesus with no special expectations, making their encounter with Him ordinary. They went away with their non-expectation fulfilled. The woman, too, had her expectation fulfilled and went away healed, proving that indeed you do get what you do or don't expect. If you expect nothing, your expectations will not be disappointed. You will leave with nothing.

Weaponisation meant that this woman made something significant of her encounter with Jesus Christ. She said, 'I must touch the hem of His garment,' thereby turning what would have been an ordinary meeting into something special. You can do the same and use anything to elicit God's powerful response in your life. One way of accomplishing that is through thanksgiving.

74

You can decide that 'God, when I am next in church, I will touch you with my praise and thanksgiving in expectation of healing, and since Jesus Christ is the same, yesterday, today, and forever, Heb 13:8, you will return home healed. You only need to come with high expectations.

Some years ago, my wife was involved in an incident on her way to work. That morning, something unusual happened before she left the house. I was upstairs when I suddenly heard a loud noise coming from downstairs. My wife was praying in tongues unusually violently, and I could only remark, 'What's going on with this woman today? Then she left for work.

Two hours later, I received a phone call informing me that she had been involved in an accident. A motorcycle courier, traveling at speed, had run into her and knocked her down as she was crossing the road to enter the hospital where she worked. The impact lifted and threw her several meters in the air, and she landed on her arm as she tried to break her fall. Thankfully, because it was winter and she was well-padded, her thick jacket provided a slight cushion that prevented skin abrasion. In the aftermath of the accident, she was taken into the hospital, checked over, prescribed some pain medicine, and discharged. She came home on her own steam. Then I understood the reason for her earlier violent prayer: God was preparing her for that encounter that Satan was readying to take her life.

After the adrenaline rush caused by the encounter had subsided, she started having pains. She had been signed off work to rest and recuperate, but was still having pains everywhere, especially in her arm. So, still in pain on Sunday morning, she contemplated missing the service and staying at home to nurse her pain. Then she heard a voice say to her, 'Where else should you go for healing but the Church?'

So, she decided to attend Sunday service. During the service, and as we were praising God, the minister said, 'I feel the presence of the Lord to heal. If you are in any kind of pain, raise your hands and worship God.' My wife, who was in pain, raised her hands and started thanking God for her healing. Then, she suddenly realised that her pain had disappeared. As Jesus would say, her faith had made her whole.

Praising and thanking God weaponised her thanksgiving, precipitating her healing. Any issue in your life that you are struggling with can be weaponised. You only must make up your mind and say, "God, as I'm going to meet you today in the church service, I expect to receive your touch." God will honour your faith.

Understand that whatever you are expecting never catches you by surprise, because it is expected. With God, the only surprise is the magnitude of what He will do for us, for He has promised to do exceedingly abundantly above all we can think or imagine by His power working in us. Ephesians 3:20

Anticipatory thanksgiving means thanking God as a seed of faith, knowing we will have a better cause to thank Him later for what He has done.

Someone who weaponised his thanksgiving to confront a hopeless situation was Prophet Habakkuk. He said "Though the fig tree may not blossom, Nor fruit be on the vines; Though the labour of the olive may fail, And the fields yield no food; Though the flock may be cut off from the fold, And there be no herd in the stalls-- Yet I will rejoice in the Lord, I will joy in the God of my salvation. The Lord God is my strength; He will make my feet like deer's feet, And He will make me walk on my high hills." Habakkuk 3:17-19

The passage above describes an extreme situation, a worst-case scenario. However, Habakkuk's response was counterintuitive the opposite of what someone in trouble would naturally do. He chose to rejoice in the face of calamity when he should have been crying and mourning in anticipation of the loss he was about to suffer.

It depicts a situation where you have no food in the house and no money to pay bills that are piling up. Your bank accounts are overdrawn, your credit cards are maxed to the limit, and the children's school fees are long overdue. The bailiffs are now banging on the door seeking to extract payments for court judgements against you. In a nutshell, you are in hot soup. So, what do you do short of killing yourself?

Your options are to play the ostrich and pretend as if everything is fine or nothing is happening; that will not work. You can also complain against God or the system and blame everyone, including yourself, for your predicament, but that still won't get you anywhere; it will probably make things worse.

What most of us in that situation would not think of doing is to thank God 'In and for everything', because it is counterintuitive to our nature. We would tend to do one of the other two options. Well, Habakkuk went for the third and nuclear option; he chose to rejoice in his troubles, confident that God would deliver him and turn things around for him and thus exposing the rationale for his non-conformist response to difficulties – God.

Habakkuk knew that so long as God is with you, it does not matter what is against you. His priority was to please the God who can help him, regardless of whose ox is gored. He understood that his opinion on the issue does not matter, and his feelings are unimportant. The only important thing is to exalt God and acknowledge His suzerainty over his life and circumstances. So, what gave Habakkuk confidence that God would act to deliver him?

Habakkuk was a servant of God. So, he knew that he belonged to God and was an instrument in His hands. So, when you know that you are a weapon of warfare, you know that you are in God's hands, and God will take care of you and use you for His glory. Consequently, you don't look at circumstances, but focus on God, the author and the finisher of your faith, confident that He who began the work in you is faithful to complete it.

David said, "I will lift up mine eyes to the hills, from whence comes my help! My help comes from the Lord, who made heaven and earth." Psalm 121:1-2 So, when you have a situation that ordinarily should put you down, that is a time to start thanking God. You weaponise your thanksgiving by rejoicing in the Lord and refusing to allow your circumstances to master you or pull you down, a sentiment reflected in Job 22:29, which states, "When they cast you down, and you say, 'Exaltation will come!' Then He will save the humble person."

Hence, the fact that you lost your job should not depress you. Weaponise your joblessness by acclaiming God as your source. Job exemplified that reality when, in one day, he went from being a millionaire to a pauper. He woke up one day, having everything, but went to bed having nothing. How did Job respond to the calamity that befell him? By saying, 'The Lord giveth, the Lord taketh. Blessed be the name of the Lord.' That single action guaranteed Job's victory.

By choosing not to complain but to glorify God in his difficulties, Job was saying, "God, this is not my problem. It is yours. Job was blessing God and thanking Him in defiance of the dictates of his circumstances.

So, when the Bible says, 'In everything, give thanks,' it means that you give thanks both in the bad and the good situations. In whatever situation you find yourself, always treat it as an opportunity to thank God.

Another kind of thanksgiving is reflectory thanksgiving. To reflect means to think about past events. Reflectory thanksgiving means reminiscing on God's goodness to help you appreciate His greatness. The Bible says, "Then King David went in and sat before the LORD; and he said: "Who am I, O Lord GOD? And what is my house, that You have brought me this far?" 2 Samuel 7:18 It is when you talk to God and God talks to you, as David did. He acknowledged that God made him and saw how far he had taken him – from nothing to becoming the king of a nation.

A Yoruba language saying states that he who thinks deeply and reflects will have cause to thank God. For many of us, our thinking is so shallow that we are always focused on what God has not done. 'God, I asked for a house, but you have not given it to me.' Yes, God might not have given you a house, but did you go to the toilet without any issue this morning? Were you able to move without assistance when you woke up? Remember that some people require help to do the simplest things, and you are no better than they are. Can you raise your hand at will and without thinking? Understand that not everyone enjoys that privilege? Do you know that some people can't raise their hands even if they want to? You said, "Oh, I plan to be in church on Sunday." And you came, and you don't see it as a privilege? Many people had the same plan as you but never made it.

Many of us take God for granted. So, by reflecting and looking deep into our lives, we start to appreciate the small things that make life worthwhile and see the greatness of God. Reflection helps us to put things in the right perspective. You will see God up there, and your problem down here, and realise that your problem is nothing compared to God, and that gives you the confidence that God will take care of you. You can then thank God.

Celebratory thanksgiving, implies celebrating and rejoicing what God has done in your life: 'This is my testimony!' 'God did this for me.' 'God gave this to me. Celebratory thanksgiving is the kind of thanksgiving that we are all familiar with. All of us have done it at one point in time for various reasons to celebrate and appreciate God's goodness in our lives.

So, how do you weaponise your thanksgiving, whatever its form? An example that will suffice is the Bible story chronicling the exploits of the Apostolic team consisting of Paul and Silas.

God had dramatically led them through the territory of modern-day Turkey or Türkiye into Greece, thereby taking the gospel to Europe from Asia Minor. As the were preaching the gospel in the city of Philippi, a demon-possessed woman started following them. She kept trying to ingratiate herself with Paul's team to confuse ordinary people about the relatedness of the spirit of divination controlling her and the Holy Spirit in whose power Paul and his team operated. Had she succeeded in her plan, the people would have struggled to differentiate between Paul's God and her demons, and the Gospel message would have been neutralised. Paul saw the danger of what she was doing and put a stop to it by casting out the demon.

However, this woman was a slave, and her gift of divination was a money earner for her masters. Angered at their loss of means of livelihood, they stirred up the people and attacked Paul and Silas, accusing them of causing trouble. The authorities did not even ask any questions, but just took them and put them in jail, even though they had not done anything wrong.

Life can sometimes be unkind to us. People can attack you even when you have done nothing wrong, and doing the right thing is no protection; they will still attack you. The sense of injustice can even be more pronounced if you were acting in obedience to God's directive, for it makes you wonder what God was doing when people were attacking you, after He had led you into it.

So, what would you have expected Paul and Salas to have done as a response to being unjustly jailed for something they were innocent of? You probably would have said, "Ah, God, I thought you sent me here. Why am I going through all this?" Paul and Silas understood what it meant to weaponise their thanksgiving. The Bible says that 'At midnight, Paul and Silas raised their voices to God and sang hymns of praise, and everybody heard them. Acts 16:25 It also implies that as they were praising God in their pain, that is, anticipatory and reflectory thanksgiving, t attracted God's presence into their predicament, and God delivered them. Thenceforth, their praise turned celebratory.

In honour of their thanksgiving, the God who inhabits the praises of His people, Psalm 22:3, showed up in power, and broke their shackles. The prison gates swung open, and the inmates were potentially free to escape, all because Paul and Silas weaponised their thanksgiving. If you desire a similar experience, you only need to follow their example and thank God like you've never done before.

Apostle Paul said, let this mind be in you which was in Christ Jesus. What mind was that? The same thanksgiving mindset Jesus had that precipitated His exploits. When Jesus Christ was about to die, He shared communion with His disciples and gave thanks. Understand that, according to Jesus' model, thanksgiving always precipitates a miracle.

The greatest miracle that Jesus Christ ever performed was raising the corpse of the 4-day-old-dead and already stinking Lazarus back to life. Even his own sisters pleaded with Jesus, 'Master, let him be.' When Lazarus was alive, he was something. But in death, he became nothing. They contended, 'Master, if only you had come earlier, our brother would still be alive.' Their understanding was that Jesus had the power to heal the sick, but was not powerful enough to raise the dead, and that was their limitation.

Hence, the principal reason you should thank God in everything is that you don't know everything. You only know in part. Thanksgiving provides a rare opportunity to experience God in a new way and know Him better and understand His agenda for our lives.

God's reason for allowing Paul and Silas to be thrown in jail despite their innocence soon became clear when the Jailer, who had been startled awake by the earthquake, discovered that the prison gates had been thrown wide open. Surmising that all the prisoners had escaped, he resolved to kill himself. Paul had to stop him by shouting, "Oh, don't harm yourself. We are all here." No one had escaped, because they too were terrified of Paul's God.

Do you know what the jailer said in response? He asked, "What must I do to be saved?" What a loaded statement! It meant that the jailer was not a stranger to the gospel. He probably had seen Paul and Silas preaching in the market, and had listened to their message and concluded that they were fools, but the moment he saw the power of God in action, the Holy Spirit convicted him of his sin, and he responded, "I am a sinner. What must I do to be saved?"

The enemy will bring trouble into your life, intending to turn you against God, but through thanksgiving, you can turn the tables on him by not playing his game. You allow God to take control of the situation and fashion out His will for you.

So, understand that when the Bible says, 'In everything', God meant 'in everything'. Even as things are falling on top of us, we still say, 'Thank you, Lord.' Hence, don't let anything trouble you, because that is what the devil wants to do to you; he wants to trouble you. Refuse to be anxious. Look fear in the eye and choose to have faith in God's ability to deliver you. You may not be able to control what happens around you, but you certainly can control what goes on in your mind. Choose to believe in God. Then, by faith, you can give thanks to God in whatever situation you find yourself, and He will come through for you.

5

Thanksgiving: Strength Through Joy

We've looked at how we can weaponise our thanksgiving, how thanksgiving helps to keep us in the will of God, and understand God's will for our lives.

In this final chapter, we will examine the secret power that enables us to fulfil and obey God's command that, "In everything give thanks, for this is the will of God for you in Christ Jesus." 1 Thessalonians 5:18

As previously mentioned, we will not always feel like thanking God. Sometimes, it is simple, especially when things are going well for you, and you want to share your testimony of God's goodness, such as when God has blessed you, your child has just graduated or married, or God has answered your prayers, or you want to give thanks to God for the fruit of the womb.

However, giving thanks can sometimes also be a battle. What if you have just lost your job? Are you going to say, 'Lord, I thank you because you've caused me to be sad? That doesn't sound right. The Bible says that God oversees our lives. He knows when you got sacked. He knew when that sack letter was being prepared, and He didn't intervene. So, you can, on one level, justifiably accuse

God that He is guilty of causing your sacking and may not feel like thanking God in that kind of situation.

Our objective is to explore how we can give thanks in and for everything, and the key to achieving that feat is joy, specifically, the joy of the Lord. So, what is joy? In Philippians 4:4, Apostle Paul wrote, 'Rejoice in the Lord always and again I say rejoice.' Combining the two passages produces, 'In everything, give thanks, for this is the will of God for you in Christ Jesus,' and 'Rejoice in the Lord always, and again I say rejoice.' You have your answer as to how you are to give thanks in everything. You are to rejoice in the Lord always.

Hence, the key to being able to give thanks to God in everything is our joy. If you can hold on to your joy, you can keep spiritually sharp and shining and will be able to rejoice in every situation. You will also realise that it will save you a lot of trouble and direct you on the right path.

As it is with everything in life, your attitude determines your altitude. Joy is the means God uses to hold our attitude in the right place. Our attitude is important because it determines how we see life. So, if everything you see is always negative, it is because you have the wrong perspective. You will have a lot of trouble with God, and probably with men also, because your attitude shows what is in your heart and influences your actions. That is why we are always encouraged to have a positive attitude in whatever we do.

Joy gives you the right perspective on life that enables you to cultivate the right attitude for your situation. Understand that apart from our salvation, joy is your next best asset. That is why Satan always aims to steal our joy from us.

Whenever the enemy attacks you, the one prize he is after is to steal your joy, and the moment he succeeds, your life is left wide open because joy is your first line of defence against enemy attacks. Hence, the reason the Bible says, 'Rejoice always' is not necessarily because things are going well for you, but that God is good, and He is for you.

So, the key to being able to stand before God and man to glorify God is understanding what it means to rejoice in the Lord always. However, there are different kinds of rejoicing. The Bible says that God rejoices over us with singing. Zephaniah 3:17 It also says that "For as a young man marries a virgin, So shall your sons marry you; And as the bridegroom rejoices over the bride, So shall your God rejoice over you." Isaiah 62:5 The kind of rejoicing that serves as a key to our victory is to rejoice in the Lord.

Just rejoicing is different from rejoicing in the Lord, for in the latter, we make God the focus of our attention and look up to Him as our deliverer. That is the key to our being victorious. Hence, our attitude is important.

An example of someone who had the wrong attitude, which God warned him about, was Cain. "But for Cain and his offering, he had no respect or regard." So Cain was exceedingly angry and indignant, and he looked sad and depressed." Genesis 4:5

This passage describes how Cain felt when God rejected him. He was angry with God, sad, and depressed. Cain was a joyless man. He had an attitude problem. Whenever somebody is depressed, it is because they lack joy. When your joy is overflowing, you don't even know how to be depressed. But, in the case of Cain, that was exactly how he felt – depressed.

"And the Lord said to Cain, 'Why are you angry? Why do you look sad and depressed, and dejected?" God's retort to Cain was, "What have I said or done to you that makes you so sullen? I only rejected what you gave to me because your heart was not right.' However, instead of Cain acting on God's suggestion and rectifying his wrong, he chose to be angry with God.

We, too, sometimes query God asking, 'Why did you allow such a thing to happen to me? We don't know if God allowed it because He wanted to teach us something new and open our eyes to things we didn't know before. So, Cain was angry with God and was querying, 'God, why did you reject my offering?' Proverbs 19:3 states, "The foolishness of a man twists his way, And his heart frets against the LORD."

Now listen to what God said in verse 7. He says, "If you do well, will you not be accepted?" Please take note of that phrase, "If you do well." What does it mean to do well? It means that if you do what you are supposed to do in that situation, will it not be well with you?

This implies that what you do or don't do when faced with challenging situations will determine God's response to you. Your response to challenges will determine how God will respond to you. Interestingly, God did not say, 'Okay, Cain, I will help you', thereby accepting responsibility for the latter's actions. Instead, He said, 'If you do well', implying that Cain was responsible for his actions.

That leads us to the second point that God always holds us responsible for our attitude and whatever actions it leads to. Cain was angry with God, but God did not say, "Okay, don't worry. I'll forgive you about this." God said, "Ah, I hold you responsible. If you do well and do what you're supposed to do, you won't be where you are now. So, do the right thing, and everything will be well with you.'

So, understand that when the Bible says, 'In everything, give thanks,' it means that God expects you to do the right thing, and that right thing is to follow the word of God concerning your life. Hence, thanksgiving is always the right thing.

Hear what God said to Cain, "And if you do not do well." God was laying down the available options to Cain: Do well, or don't. He said, 'But if you do not do well, sin crouches at your door."

The enemy's goal in attacking us is to steal our joy and turn us against God. He wants us to blame God for our predicament and make God angry with us. He wants to cut us off from our source so that he can further entrench himself into our lives, and he will succeed if we do not do well.

God's warning to Cain is, "Don't do that. You will fall into Satan's trap." Being pig-headed and insisting on going our own way can lead us into Satan's trap. Yes, you can say, "Well, God, you are in charge of my life. You are the owner of my life. You won't allow anything bad to happen to me. You said that your plans for me are of good and not of evil to give me an expected end." Jeremiah 29:11 And God's response is, "Yeah, all those things are true, but you are still responsible for your actions. If you think I'm failing you, I still hold you accountable for your attitude. How you treat me is how I will treat you.'

Do you complain about your situation and thus highlight God's seeming and implied incompetence? Or do you say, 'God, I don't know what is going on, but you are still my God.' So, you have a choice, and God is now saying that if you do not do well, sin is crouching at your door.

This implies that sin is stalking you like a predator stalks its prey. The word 'Crouch' means to adopt a position where the knees are bent and the upper body is brought forward and down, typically to avoid detection or to defend oneself: it is to hide in preparation to pounce. God's warning to Cain was that Satan is always monitoring and seeking to leverage your poor attitude against you. The converse is that God is also constantly surveilling your attitude to gauge if you are deserving of His blessing.

So, if all God sees you doing is complaining and denigrating Him, He will restrain His help, and that opens the door for the devil to pounce and hurt you. Satan instigates us to complain against a seeming lack of care because he wants us to sin and give him access to our lives to occasion our ruin.

Whenever you are faced with challenges or experience temptation, understand that sin is always crouching and lying in wait for you to make the wrong choice to occasion your fall. God's escape plan for you is that if you do the right thing at that crucial time, sin will not have power or dominion over you.

So, what is that thing we must do to avoid falling under the power of the devil? The Bible says, 'Rejoice'. Specifically, 'Rejoice in the Lord always.' That is how you resist the devil and force him to flee from you. James 4:7

Hear Apostle James' take on the issue. He said, "My brethren, count it all joy when you fall into various trials, knowing that the testing of your faith produces patience. But let patience have its perfect work, that you may be perfect and complete, lacking nothing." James 1:2-4 Joy is your defence and key to your victory.

If you can learn and understand this important spiritual truth, it does not mean that you will never face challenges again in your life. I guarantee that you will. However, I can also guarantee that if you decide to always do the right thing, you will have more opportunities to fulfil your destiny, because your life will honour God. That is the reason the joy of the Lord is the key to fulfilling your destiny.

So, what is joy? Joy is a component of the fruit of the Holy Spirit and the outworking of God's character in us. Joy is different from happiness, although both have the attribute of gladness. Happiness is subject to our circumstances - winning the lottery makes you happy. Why? Because something good has happened to you, and it can be positively life changing. Losing your job makes you sad because something bad has happened to you.

Joy is different from happiness because it is what God has placed within you and is therefore not subject to your environment. Hence, as Christians, all of us have joy in us. The issue is whether you activate that joy and make it work for you.

So, how do we know that we have joy in us? Because it is the fruit of the Spirit. If you are born again, that is, the Spirit bears witness with your spirit that you are a child of God, Romans 8:16, then you have His joy potentially in you. It is as you yield to the leading of the Holy Spirit that your joy starts to manifest and impact your life.

Galatians 5:22-23 states, "But the fruit of the Spirit is love, joy, peace, longsuffering, kindness, goodness, faithfulness, gentleness, self-control. Against such there is no law." So, all these attributes are already within us because the Holy Spirit is working within us. You already have joy as a seed, but you must make up your mind to exercise your will and rejoice to spur your joy into life and cause it to overflow.

Understand that you have the innate ability to exercise your will. It is your right as a human being and free moral agent created in the image of God. The Bible says in Habakkuk 3:17-19, "Though the fig tree may not blossom, Nor fruit be on the vines; Though the labour of the olive may fail, And the fields yield no food; Though the flock may be cut off from the fold, And there be no herd in the stalls-- Yet I will rejoice in the Lord, I will joy in the God of my salvation. The Lord God is my strength; He will make my feet like deer's feet, And He will make me walk on my high hills."

Habakkuk's situation was as bad as it could get; it was the worst-case scenario, and the embodiment of Murphy's Law. Everything that could go wrong had already gone wrong and looked seemingly unsalvageable. Yet, his response was, "I will rejoice."

So, it comes back to you. It is your responsibility, your choice, what you do with what you have. You determine and say, 'Where I am concerned, I choose to rejoice. It is first a choice to rejoice; then it translates into an action. What happens next is that the spirit of joy will fill you as God releases the spirit of joy to fill and overflow through you.

The mechanism of action is that our decision usually translates into action, and then the spirit takes over. For example, the Bible says, "And since we have the same spirit of faith, according to what is written, "I believed and therefore I spoke," we also believe and therefore speak." 2 Corinthians 4:13 This implies that as you choose faith and act in faith, God will impart the Spirit of faith that makes our faith unassailable.

What started as an act of the will is translated by the spirit of faith into the outworking of the Holy Spirit in us. Speaking words of faith elicits the release of God's power to bring about their fulfilment. So, you are no longer forcing yourself to exercise your faith; it just comes naturally because God has taken over and is empowering you. Your faith then soars to a level where it can achieve its objective.

Joy operates on the same spiritual format because, like faith, it already exists in our hearts in a small measure as a fruit of the Spirit. So, when you decide through the force of will that, 'God, I will rejoice, and follow your decision with active rejoicing, God will impart the Spirit of joy that will translate the nature of your joy from contrived to effortless. This enables you to draw from the well of strength that is God's power to meet your needs.

Hence, the key to attaining victory over your circumstances is to choose to rejoice in the Lord, but why do you want to rejoice in the Lord? It is because God is a known quantity. He does not change; He cannot lie; He cannot die. He will never turn His back on you. He is so solid and therefore always dependable. That confidence you have in Him is the reason you can say, "God, even if everything is not going well for me, I know that you are still in control of our life and will cause all things to work together for my good." Knowing that God does not change enables you to exercise faith in Him.

In response to your faith, God will release His power upon you and start making what you thought was impossible possible. Joy follows the same format. Your rejoicing will empower God to act in your life and open doors of opportunity that you never knew were there.

However, also understand that by the same token, your lack of joy and complaining can cause you to turn against God or turn God against you, which was Satan's evil intent for you. He wants to cut you off from God and isolate you. It opens the door of mischief for the enemy to attack you, because as God warned Cain, sin is always crouching at your door, seeking to pounce on you and occasion your fall.

So, whenever you feel tempted to complain, just say, "God, I know that this will cause me to sin against you. I refuse to do it. Instead, I will do the right thing as prescribed in your word, which says, "In everything, give thanks." 'So,

I thank you. Even though I don't feel like it, I shall fake it till I make it, because I know that as I praise and exalt you, you shall pour your oil of joy on me. The Spirit of joy shall fill me.' The Bible says, "You love righteousness and hate wickedness; Hence God, Your God, has anointed you with the oil of gladness more than Your companions." Psalm 45:7

When you open your life to God by rejoicing in the Lord, you prove to Him that you love righteousness and hate wickedness. God will respond to your faithfulness by anointing you with the oil of gladness or joy, and His joy will overshadow you and become your strength, empowering you to do all things in Christ, who strengthens you. Keep this truth in mind, because you will need it one day.

The only exception when joy doesn't work as we might expect is when it has God's agenda is attached to it. This means God is working to the dictates of a bigger picture than we can imagine, but would, in the fullness of time, honour His commitment to us to fill us with joy overflowing.

Although God expects us to rejoice always, Job was one man who rejoiced in his calamity but failed to experience the immediate impact of his joy. When calamity befell him, how did Job respond? He bowed down in worship and said, 'The Lord giveth, the Lord taketh. Blessed be the name of the Lord.' Job did what was right about his circumstances, but it had no immediate impact on his situation.

Job, therefore, initially proved the only exception to the norm that when you do the right thing by praising and glorifying God, it shall be well with you.

Ultimately, God came through for him, as He caused Job's joy to become full and overflowing. God blessed and compensated Job with double for the troubles he suffered

When you fight to keep your joy and stop the enemy from stealing your heritage of joy and source of divine strength, God will honour you with His presence and put an end to Satan's attack on you, for His word assures us that in His presence, is fullness of joy, and at His right hand are pleasure forevermore. Psalm 16:11 This proves that God's presence is the primary requirement for overflowing joy.

So, if your question is, 'Why have I been rejoicing in the Lord, but nothing has been happening?' It is clearly because God has an agenda that impacts the timing and nature of His response. After going through a wringer of an experience, Job finally revealed God's agenda in Job 42:5 by saying, "I have heard of you by the hearing of the ear, but now my eyes see you." Before understanding God's agenda for his life, Job laboured under the assumption that he knew God. He concluded that he could have known Him better, and he now does.

None of us, when asked, 'Do you know God?' would answer, "No." We all know God but know Him in different ways and to different degrees. So, whenever God wants to reveal more of Himself to us, He might choose to temporarily suspend or withdraw the blessing that we've been enjoying for a while so that we can see the other side of life and thus appreciate Him more. That was what happened to Job.

Although he praised God and rejoiced in the Lord, God still delayed Job's deliverance until he had received the revelation God intended for him. That led Job to realise that perfect love casts out fear. Job finally saw the flaw God saw in him: the fact that up till the time of his calamity, he was being ruled by an inordinate fear of God.

Job's statement in response to his calamity was, 'That which I feared has come upon me'. His statement after his trial was that "I have heard of you by the hearing of the ear, but now my eyes see you.' Job 42:5. Knowing God banished Job's fears and perfected his walk with God, making Job a better person and a mature follower of God. Like Job, God's agenda for our lives is always good to perfect our expectations of Him.

Joy, like thanksgiving, is a seed. By choosing to rejoice in the Lord, you are sowing and nurturing your seed of thanksgiving. The Law of harvest dictates that you reap in multiples of joy. Doing the right thing, i.e., rejoicing in the Lord, protects you from straying from the right path or enables you to reverse course if you have strayed.

Doing the right thing is a matter of obedience and not feelings. It means saying, 'God, I choose to praise you. I thank you in this situation.' Even though things are hard, rejoicing in the Lord stops the enemy from gaining access or making further inroads into your life, and if you've gone your way but decided to do right thing and say, 'Lord, I don't know how I got here, but I choose to bless you', God will ensure that His blessing enables you to get back on track.

I have shared my story of how I became depressed because things were not going well for me. What I later discovered was that so long as I focused on God, the situation was manageable. The joy of the Lord was springing forth from my heart, and I couldn't care less how difficult my situation was.

Things changed for me the moment I allowed myself to be distracted and started asking, 'God, why is everything going well for everybody except me? Instead of thanking God as Scripture dictates, I started complaining about my situation and subsequently fell into sin. Satan, who had been crouching, patiently waiting for his opportunity to attack me, pounced on me with relish and afflicted me with depression.

The following Sunday morning, I chose to lie on my bed rather than prepare to attend the Church service. I would normally be one of the first people to open the church doors and get everything ready. While hiding under the duvet, God spoke to me and asked me, 'David, what are you doing here?' I knew I had no business lying in bed on a Sunday morning when I should have been serving in God's house, and I felt convicted in my spirit.

Knowing I was wrong, I asked forgiveness of God and requested that He get me out of the depression that had entangled me, promising that I would never allow myself to be in that situation again. I took responsibility for my sin, and God gave me the grace to overcome depression. It's been over thirty years since that episode, and I have been in tougher situations since, but I have never been depressed. God has kept me by His grace, and I am now wiser; I am determined not to fall for the crouching devil of depression again.

So, understand that even when you've strayed from God, His joy will get you back on track, because rejoicing in the Lord always is the right thing to do. So long as you have God at the centre of your life, it doesn't matter what may be going on around you. The enemy always wants to distract you, steal your joy and dissipate your strength. He will show you what God has not done, and the things that are not going well in your life, because he wants to convince you that focusing on God is not the best for you.

Understand that Satan is a liar and the father of lies. John 8:44 So, refuse to play his game, and say, 'Lord, my eyes are on you, and I'm not moving them, not even one inch. I will keep them focused on you.' Taking his eyes off Jesus Christ was the only mistake Peter made as he walked on water, and consequently, he began to sink. Matthew 14:28-29

Peter had challenged Jesus Christ as the latter came walking on water towards His disciples, 'Master, if it is you, bid me to come.' Jesus' one-word response was, 'Come.' Peter immediately leapt out of the boat and landed on, and not in, the water. To his surprise, the water bore his weight. Peter gingerly walked towards Jesus but was concerned about the billowing waves. Then he realised what was going on and began to doubt. At that moment, he also started sinking and cried out to Jesus to save him. Jesus stretched forth His hand and lifted Peter up, but with a stern rebuke, 'Why did you doubt?'

Fear and doubt overtook Peter when he lost his focus on God. So, to avoid doubt, keep your eyes on God. Yes, your marriage may be going through a rough patch, but don't focus on your spouse. Keep your eyes on God. Your children may be rebellious, but don't focus on them. Keep your eyes on God because that is how you float and walk upon even the worst of life's stormy seas and not sink. Trusting in God will enable you to rejoice in difficulties because your eyes are on God. You are too focused on God to be distracted by the devil's antics. With God, you always have hope that shines a light in your darkness.

Years ago, a group of scientists experimented by placing a mouse in a tin containing water. Then, they shut the lid in such a way that the mouse could receive air but not light. A few minutes later, they opened the lid and found the mouse drowned.

They repeated the same experiment but with one significant difference: they bored a hole on top of the lid to allow light into the tin. 72 hours later, the mouse was still alive. Why? Because that light was a ray of hope that something might happen and kept the mouse struggling for its life.

Joy serves the same purpose to us as the light did for that mouse. It enables you to maintain your hope in God. That was why David questioned himself, "Why are you cast down, O my soul? And why are you disquieted within me? Hope in God; For I shall yet praise Him, the help of my countenance and my God." Psalm 42:11

You are rejoicing now in difficulties because you know that a time will come when you rejoice in celebration, but to get to that successful end, you must necessarily keep your eyes focused on God. The Bible says, 'Delight yourself in the Lord, and he shall give you the desires of your heart. Psalm 37:4 By thanking God, you are telling God, 'I intend to make you happy, regardless of how I feel and whatever it costs me. Prioritising God above our feelings delights Him and causes Him to be delighted in us. This is what happens when God delights in us: "When the Lord delights in the way of a man, He makes his footsteps firm. Though he stumbles, he will not fall, because the Lord will uphold him.' Psalm 37:23

So, if the Lord delights in you and you delight in God, it doesn't mean that you will not face challenges. However, understand that because you have God on your side the victory is already yours to appropriate, because the joy of the Lord is your strength.

Hence, we give thanks in everything by rejoicing in the Lord always and steadfastly refusing to focus on our circumstances but instead riveting our eyes on God. Satan will tempt you to take your eyes off God, but don't fall for it. Once you have exercised your will by saying, 'I will rejoice in the Lord God of my salvation. I will thank the Lord.' You must continue to thank Him. Don't let the enemy stop you. Don't complain that 'No matter what I do, nothing seems to be changing.'

By thanking God in everything, you have already invited God into your life, thereby guaranteeing His presence. You have authorised and are allowing God to do whatever is necessary to deliver your victory. Remember that God's presence implies the fullness of joy. Hence, it is only a matter of time till your joy starts to overflow.

So, why will God respond to your thanksgiving? It is because thanksgiving or rejoicing in the Lord is the perfect will of God for your life. You can never go wrong. That's why the Bible says rejoice in the Lord always, and in everything, give thanks. Whatever the circumstances, and however bad things may be, resolve to thank God in the spirit of obedience, because it is His will for your life.

So, if anybody asks, 'Are you one of those radical people who are always thanking God in everything? Say, 'Yes, I am.' Because you now understand that thanksgiving is God's will for your life. I faltered when directly challenged with that question several decades ago by somebody I respected, but I know better now.

Back then I didn't have a full understanding of what thanksgiving meant, probably because I was just starting my journey seeking to know God through praise and thanksgiving. Now, with the knowledge and experience since gained, I can confidently say that I am one of those who thank God in everything and rejoice in the Lord always. Why? Because it is the will of God.

I will conclude by quoting David's words. He says, "Whoever offers praise glorifies Me; And to him who orders his conduct aright I will show the salvation of God." Psalm 50:23

Thanksgiving sets us up to do the right thing, thereby empowering God to deliver His salvation to us in our troubles. So, thank God in everything.

OTHER PUBLICATIONS BY THE AUTHOR:

MAKING GOD'S BLESSINGS COUNT

ISBN 0-9548763-0-X (9780954876309)

In this book you will learn how to:

- Develop the quantum leap of faith that is essential to possessing your inheritance: How to

  ➢ Make effective and intelligent prayer
  ➢ Develop your faith from scratch
  ➢ Effectively deploy your faith.
  ➢ Reason yourself to greater faith by applying the logic of faith
  ➢ Develop lasting faith and faith for the impossible

- Open your mouth wide in faith as you make use of your spiritual authority: How to

  ➢ Pray with boldness
  ➢ Understand the power of His name

- ➢ Appropriate the innate power of words
- ➢ Offer prayers without limit
- ➢ Make today's confessions tomorrow's realities

- Partake of the children's bread, which consists of God's provision for His people. It addresses the issues -

  - ➢ Who are the spiritual dogs?
  - ➢ The children's bread
  - ➢ The bread of affliction
  - ➢ Cast your bread
  - ➢ Our divine portion
  - ➢ The secret of abundance
  - ➢ The true riches

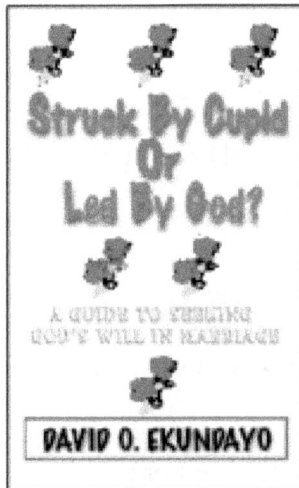

STRUCK BY CUPID OR LED BY GOD?
(A Guide To Seeking God's Will In Marriage)

ISBN: 0-9548763-1-8 (9780954876319)

Your ability as a Christian and as an individual to fulfil God's plan and purpose for your life depends on choosing the right partner.

This book contains spiritual insights that could prove an invaluable help in finding not only the right spouse, but also God's purpose for your life. In fact, it could change the direction of your life for all eternity.

In this book you will learn:

- The importance of involving God in your choice of a marriage partner.
- The purpose of marriage.
- How to deal with the issue and temptation of close proximity relationship with the opposite sex.
- How to identify a genuine Christian.
- How to listen to God's voice.
- How to conduct the four tests that would help clarify your choice of a marriage partner.
- How to have courtship without tears.
- How to influence your child's choice of a marriage partner and secure your heritage for generations.
- Spirit-empowered singleness.

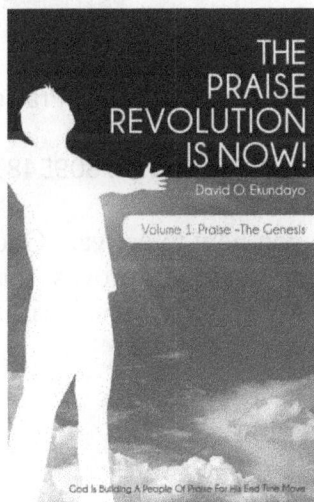

The Praise Revolution Is Now! Vol 1 Praise: The Genesis

ISBN: 09548763-3-4 (9780954876333)

- This book will teach you how to activate God's eternal covenant with His children through praise. It proves that the reality of divine protection and provision can be yours. Learn how praise is the key to experiencing the fullness of God.

The Praise Revolution Is Now! Vol 2 Praise: The Covenant

ISBN: 09548763-4-2 (9780954876340)

- This book will teach you how to activate God's eternal covenant with His children through praise. It proves that the reality of divine protection and provision can be yours. Learn how praise is the key to experiencing the fullness of God.

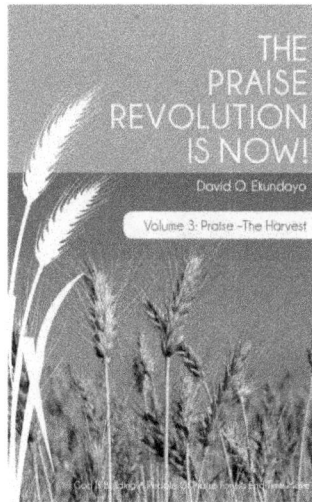

The Praise Revolution Is Now! Vol 3 Praise: The Harvest

ISBN: 09548763-5-0 (9780954876357)

- This final book in the series explores the role of praise in the end time move of God as well as its implication for you. It is a must read if your desire is to see God move in a new way in your life.